THE INVENTION OF THE SPECTATOR

FRÉDÉRIC GIMELLO-MESPLOMB

THE INVENTION OF THE SPECTATOR

How has early film spectatorship shaped audience and reception theory

Selected Writings (1910-1920)

Text and cover illustration: OpenCulture Academic Publishing
Typographic design and layout: Derek Murphy and Reedsy
Find our catalog at http://openculture.fr/
Contact: infos@culturea.fr

ISBN paperback : 9791043111785
ISBN e-book : 9791043111785
Legal deposit: december 2024

First Printing, 2024

This book supports Plantons Pour l'Avenir, an endowment fund for the reforestation of French forests. More than 400 forest reforestation projects supported since 2014 across France. https://www.plantonspourlavenir.fr/

Acknowledgments

The author is grateful for helpful discussions with a number of graduate students and faculty members in the Department of Information and Communication Sciences at Avignon University (France).

"The Bioscope" extracts and quotations are with permission. The Bioscope was a blog on early and silent cinema, with an emphasis on research and audience studies active in the early 2010's. The Bioscope is no longer active, but you can find on its online archive nearly 1,400 posts on all aspects of silent film published from February 2007 to August 2012.

The author also acknowledges :

Abderrahim Benslimane, Djazaira Berkouk, Olivier Blaise, Bérénice Bonhomme, Colin Burnett, Bruno Caillé, Jean Cluzel, Morgan Corriou, Jean-Pierre Costa, Laurent Creton, Jean Davallon, Jean-François Diana, Jean-Louis Dufour, Isabelle Duval, Jean-Yves Le Déhaut, Emmanuel Ethis, Jean-Louis Fabiani, Anika Falkert, Maristella Fatichenti, Carole Faure, Sandrine Fdida, Mathieu Feryn, Béatrice Fleury, Christlord Foreste, Marie-Pierre Fourquet-Courbet, Edyta Galecka, Cyrielle Garson, Sébastien Genvo, Madelena Gonzalez, Hana Gottesdiener, Philippe Goudard, Roxane Hamery, So-Hee Han, Guy Hebeler, Jean-Marc Huart,

François Hurard, Laurent Jullier, Serge Kauffmann, Kira Kitsopanidou, Pascal Laborderie, Paul Lacoste, Claire Lahuerta, Bernard Lamizet, Emmanuel Laurentin, Hélène Laurichesse, Jean-Marc Leveratto, Stéphanie Louis, Vincent Lowy, Nathalie Macé, Sophie Malbec, Damien Malinas, Luc Massou, Sarah Matelot, Philippe Met, Charlie Michael, Nolwen Mingant, Frédéric Monier, Fabrice Montebello, Mohamed Morchid, Pierre Morelli, Olivier Moëschler, Jammie Gnoc Nguyen, Giang Pen N'Guyen, Richard Barton Palmer, Emmanuel Pedler, Milica Pejanovic, Nicolas Pelissier, Frank Petit, Sandra Poitevin, Katalin Pôr, Daniel Raichvarg, Graham Ranger, Paola Ranzini, Paul Rasse, Linda Ravez, Franck Renucci, Anthony Rescigno, Florence Robine, Fabrice Rochelandet, Anne-Florence Rémy, Eric Sanjuan, Mariana Medeiros Seixas, Brigitte Simonot, Sophie Taillan, Christel Taillibert, Olivier Thévenin, Jean-Christophe Vilatte, Ana Vinuela, Jacques Walter, JianLin Wei, Dominique Wolton, Hervé Zénouda

Garbo still belongs to that moment in cinema when capturing the human face still plunged audiences into the deepest ecstasy, when one literally lost oneself in a human image as one would in a philtre, when the face represented a kind of absolute state of the flesh, which could be neither reached nor renounced.

— "The Face of Garbo," Mythologies (1957), trans. Annette Lavers [Farrar, Straus (1986, pg. 56)

Roland Barthes

Contents

Foreword

THE 1910s : PIONEERING INSIGHTS INTO CINEMA AUDIENCES STUDIES

Frédéric Gimello-Mesplomb

This book endeavors to unearth the earliest texts, often overlooked or obscure, about the discourse on cinema audiences. We aspire to challenge the prevailing notion that views these pioneering texts from the pre-1920s era as rudimentary attempts, primarily focused on either compiling lists of cinema spectators or delineating their socio-demographic profiles. Contrary to this perception, we aim to demonstrate that these initial writings on audiences have significantly shaped subsequent endeavors, ultimately contributing to establishing a comprehensive theory of audiences—a still delineating and defining field.

Drawing from key texts such as Elsaesser and Barker's *Early Cinema: Space, Frame, Narrative* (1990), we argue that these early efforts were deeply intertwined with the immense social, economic and cultural transformations reshaping the fabric of modern life in the late 19th and early 20th centuries. The rise of industrial capitalism, urbanization and new forms of industrial labor reorganized experiences of work and leisure in profound ways. Meanwhile, technological innovations from mass printing to photography and moving pictures gave birth to new mass media forms and consumer products catering to emerging urban populations.

In this heady milieu of social flux, the introduction of cinema sparked intense debate across many spheres. On one hand, movies were embraced by some progressive reformers as a powerful potential tool for mass education, enculturation and even social control of the working classes and new immigrant populations. Advocates highlighted cinema's ability to transmit ideas, cultural values and modes of behavior in an attractive entertainment format resonant with modern urban sensibilities.

Simultaneously, moralists and conservative voices, as discussed in Hansen's *Babel and Babylon: Spectatorship in American Silent Film* (1991), sounded alarms about movies' potential to corrupt and degrade public tastes, spur delinquency, and undermine traditional social structures - a fear particularly potent when it came to their impacts on children and lower classes seen as susceptible to such influences. Gunning (1986) suggests that early cinema was a site of negotiation, where audiences, filmmakers, and exhibitors interacted to shape the medium's conventions and possibilities.

Musser (1990) further argues that the cinema was not just a passive receptacle for the audience's gaze, but an active participant in the construction of meaning . The cinema was a space of social interaction, where audiences could engage with the film and each other, shaping the viewing experience and the film's interpretation. Staiger (2005) highlights the role of the cinema as a site of cultural exchange. The cinema was not just a place to watch films but a space where different cultures, classes, and genders could interact, negotiate, and influence each other. This aspect of the cinema experience, often overlooked in traditional film studies, is crucial to understanding the complex dynamics of early cinema audiences.

This polarized context, situated within the birth of consumer capitalism's reorganization of private and public life, spurred sociological, psychological, cultural, and even anthropological inquiries into cinema as a vital new social force and emergent moviegoing as a pattern of modern life.

Scholars across disciplines interrogated who was attending movies, why they were drawn to this new mass experience, and what psychological, ideological or behavioral effects could result.

Starting in the 1910s, pioneering academics explored this new movie audience's social composition and motivations through ethnographic methods, providing foundational studies of moviegoing habits that would lead to more complex interdisciplinary analyses during the subsequent peak periods of widespread movie attendance in the 1930s-1940s. These later landmark studies, such as the Payne Fund research, investigated how different types of films influenced the psychology, identities, worldviews, and even delinquent behavior of specific audience groups like children/adolescents or marginalized communities. Such inquiries drew on an interdisciplinary array of emergent theoretical frameworks from sociology, psychology, anthropology, and nascent communication studies.

Notable examples include the works of sociologists like Herbert Blumer (1900-1987), as well as pioneering ethnographic studies by Emilie Altenloh and the Payne Fund Studies, conducted in the 1920s-1930s, which examined the effects of movies on children and adolescents from integrated psychological, sociological, anthropological and emerging media effects perspectives (Jowett et al., 1996; Butsch, 2000).

The very coining of the terms "sociology of the cinema" and "sociology of audiences" by a handful of prescient academics in the 1910s reflected this inherently multidisciplinary approach to grappling with the new phenomenon of movies as modern life. However, this initial caution in narrating disciplinary boundaries was rapidly transcended as audience research quickly evolved in tandem with the swiftly commercializing film industry's own economic interests and the exigencies of the World War era. Early scholars' keen observations regarding nuances of audience demographics, differing reception strategies, and the commercial importance of accurately studying and incorporating spectators' desires into marketing, promotion and narrative strategies displayed a sophisticated understanding of the emerging spectatorial dynamics at play.

Groundbreaking works like Emilie Altenloh's "Zur Soziologie des Kino" (1914) mined Veblenian theories of status and leisure consumption, ethnographic methods from anthropology, and avant-garde aesthetic concepts like the "cinema of attractions" to anatomize working-class movie spectators' experiences in Mannheim. This landmark study highlighted how movies provided an affordable escape into fantasy and insight into aspirational lifestyles, theorizing their power to both subvert and reinscribe class and gender norms. Influential texts like the British Cinema Commission Report (1917) consolidated moralistic, educational, psychological and national security perspectives in assessing the social impacts of movies and regulation through censorship (Rae, 2019; Staiger, 1992).

The overarching goal of this volume is to establish a critical intellectual genealogy linking these early, interdisciplinary attempts at theorizing the new subjective experiences and social dynamics of movie spectatorship, to the subsequent canonical works and robust conceptual frameworks advanced by pioneering film theorists of the 1920s-1930s like Hugo Münsterberg, Rudolf Arnheim, Siegfried Kracauer, Walter Benjamin and others. Too often, the historiography of film theory leaps from recognizing Münsterberg's seminal 1916 psychological study "The Photoplay" to crediting the later Weimar and Frankfurt School philosophers with first grappling with cinema as a consequential modern art form worthy of rigorous aesthetics, perception theory and ideology critique.

However, this book seeks to recuperate and highlight the crucial, if underexplored, proto-theoretical groundwork and interdisciplinary foundation laid by the scattered writings, ethnographies, psychological studies, economic analyses and reception surveys produced in the 1910s by researchers across academia, industry and government. While inherently limited by their pragmatic aims and lack of coherent unifying frameworks, these hard-to-classify exploratory texts provided vital early framings of spectators' pivotal roles as active meaners in the cinematic experience. They advanced germinal theoretical concepts like the "attractions" model of viewer engagement, established methodologies for empirically studying audiences, and began articulating how movies could serve as dreamworlds channeling desires, shaping socialization, and constructing new cultural subjectivities beyond mere demographic categories.

A significant factor long obscuring these proto-theoretical contributions has been the decidedly uncanonical, "grey literature" nature of the primary sources - overwhelmingly comprised of doctoral dissertations, commissioned industry marketing surveys, educational pamphlets, local censorship rulings and limited-circulation reports by civic groups. Nevertheless, closely analyzing these first-hand records of how audiences were consuming, interpreting and even contesting movies in their initial decades reveals a rich genealogy of thought that should be engaged with and built upon by any comprehensive study of the dynamic spectatorial phenomenon, rather than treated as a mere historical preface.

Over the past half-century, academic film studies and histories of cinema have produced an immense body of invaluable scholarship tracing the technological innovations, artistic movements, industry practices, and key works and figures underlying the evolutionary development of movies into a mature mass art form and commercial behemoth. However, the intellectual history charting the diverse origins and progression of theories grappling with the spectator's changing roles and relationships to those cinematic forms has remained relatively underdeveloped. This volume aims to enrich that parallel history of spectatorship theory as an interdisciplinary trajectory uniting disciplines like aesthetic philosophy, psychology, sociology, anthropology, and political economy around the pivotal social and cultural implications of movie-going as a modern experience.

This thematic inquiry engaged pioneering thinkers in tangential fields since the 1910s, accelerating after World War 1 as movies transitioned into a dominant mass entertainment tied to new practices of commercialization, marketing, and questions of propaganda. It necessarily intersected with economic interests surrounding the rapidly-consolidating and internationalizing film industry, the technological standardizations allowing for streamlined systems of production and distribution, as well as pressing institutional issues around regulating audience access and the need to empirically study movie impacts on attitudes and behaviors.

Well before figures like Münsterberg, Walter Benjamin, or the Frankfurt School thinkers, interdisciplinary scholars had initiated research programs theorizing moviegoing habits through ethnographies and surveys, studying Hollywood marketing's appeals to spectatorial desires, analyzing censorship rulings for how they constructed systems of representation, and attempting to map cinema's ideological dimensions by examining its effects on specific demographic groups. While limited by empiricist methods, localized data sets and lack of unifying paradigms, this scattered proto-theory cumulatively displayed an emerging recognition that movies necessitated understanding the spectator's critical role in constructing experiences and meanings.

For instance, the pioneering works of figures like the poet Vachel Lindsay in "The Art of the Moving Picture" (1915) and Terry Ramsaye's seminal history "A Million and One Nights" (1926) explored cinema's artistic, cultural and industrial dimensions through the lens of emerging fan cultures and shifts in working-class leisure patterns enabled by Fordist capitalism - foreshadowing theoretical interest in ideology, reception and media's socio-economic contexts (Koszarski, 1994; Staiger, 2005).

By excavating and interweaving these historically overlooked or marginalized sources, the present volume reconstructs an archaeology of early interdisciplinary efforts to account for the subjective experiences, psychological dynamics and socio-cultural impacts of cinema as an unprecedented media-technological phenomenon provoking fascination and anxiety. Collectively, these writings by academics, educators, social critics, journalists, policymakers, and industry insiders laid the vital conceptual groundwork for theorizing the spectator's pivotal positionality and meaning-making role before such inquiries cohered into more sustained disciplinary paradigms.

The book's three-part structure illuminates how interdisciplinary strands coalesced into tendrils of audience theory:

- Part I chronicles the perceptual shift from conceiving spectators as passive recipients to recognizing their agency as interpreters actively co-creating cinematic meaning, as delineated through early script manuals, writings on visual pleasure by figures like Vachel Lindsay, and psychological studies of film's immersive effects on attention and identification.

- Part II explores how public institutions' concerns around cinema's potential social impacts catalyzed initiatives to regulate and educate audience behavior, merging discourse strands from public policy, educational theory, cultural criticism, religious censorship advocacy and other normative spheres contending with movies' semiotic construction of representations.
- Finally, Part III's case studies showcase pioneering attempts at systematic, empirical audience research transcending purely demographic surveys, as in sociological fieldwork on moviegoing cultures and studies of films' ideological functions across marginalized communities. Works like Emilie Altenloh's pathbreaking "Zur Soziologie des Kino" and the exhaustive survey "The Audience" presaged central methodologies and theoretical paradigms of later reception studies and effects research.

By critically recuperating these buried genealogies, the book elucidates how scattered, uncoordinated lines of interdisciplinary inquiry coalesced into the intellectual foundations for theories of audiences, spectatorship, subjective engagement, and reception that remain vital for comprehending the viewers' pivotal role in constructing meanings, ideologies, and identities within evolving media experiences. While inherently rudimentary, limited by empiricist methods, and lacking unifying theoretical architecture, these pre-disciplinary investigations laid the conceptual bedrock for grappling with cinema as a new modern phenomenon necessitating new analytical frameworks for the spectator's meaning-making agency as an active, interpreting subject within larger social, economic, technological and ideological matrices. Recognizing and building upon such overlooked proto-theoretical origins enriches understanding of the diverse, interdisciplinary roots informing subsequent traditions of audience and reception theory and media studies.

Prof. Frédéric Gimello-Mesplomb
Avignon, Summer 2024

Notes:

- Elsaesser, Thomas, and Adam Barker, eds. *Early Cinema: Space, Frame, Narrative*. London: BFI, 1990.
- Gunning, Tom. "The Cinema of Attraction: Early Film, Its Spectator and the Avant-Garde." *Wide Angle* 8.3/4 (1986): 63-70.
- Hansen, Miriam. *Babel and Babylon: Spectatorship in American Silent Film*. Cambridge, MA: Harvard University Press, 1991.
- Musser, Charles. *The Emergence of Cinema: The American Screen to 1907*. Berkeley: University of California Press, 1990.
- Staiger, Janet. *Media Reception Studies*. New York: NYU Press, 2005.

TOWARD AN ARCHAEOLOGY OF AUDIENCES

1

London Audiences of the Cinématographe

Although unwilling to quarrel with William Shakspere about his statement that the rose would smell as sweet under any other name, I can't help thinking that "Cinématographe" is a nasty word for busy people. It has a terrifying effect upon the man in the street who calls an entertainment a "show." But it must be confessed that, despite its name, M. Lumière's invention is one that will ultimately emulate the telegraph and telephone in usefulness. Instantaneous photography developed to a surprising extent is, apparently, the secret of the Cinématographe. Photographs of a moving scene taken at the rate of fifteen per second, and thrown on to a screen through the machine at the same rapid rate, enable the eye to retain one image until the successor is presented. The result is a moving picture of the event, scrupulously exact in detail, whose importance it would be difficult to overestimate.

The columns of *The Sketch* are my confessional, and I do not hesitate to say that its long name kept me away from the hew invention when the scribes of London were bidden to its reception.

I saw the Cinématographe worked for the first time at the Empire Theatre last Monday week. Ten pictures were presented. I take one, "The Arrival of the Paris Express," as a type. A railway-station is the subject of the first photograph thrown on the screen, and, from flashes in all directions, it is evident that the effect is sustained by rapidly continued exposures. In the distance there is some smoke, then the engine of the express is seen, and in a few seconds the train rushes in so quickly that, in common with most of the people in the front rows of the stalls, I shift uneasily in my seat and think of railway accidents. Then the train slows down and stops, passengers alight, the bustle of the station is absolutely before us the figures are life-size. Old country women ascend and descend some man jumps on to the platform, and then looks about helplessly, until other passengers elbow him aside. It is such a scene as I have often witnessed on a journey to or from the Riviera and, in the darkened house, it stands out with a realism that seemingly defies improvement. Granting, for the sake of argument, that this picture took one minute to present, it represented nine hundred photographs originally taken at the station in the same space of time, and there was no palpable break in the continuity of the series. The effect on the audience was shown by the applause that would not be silenced until the picture was presented again.

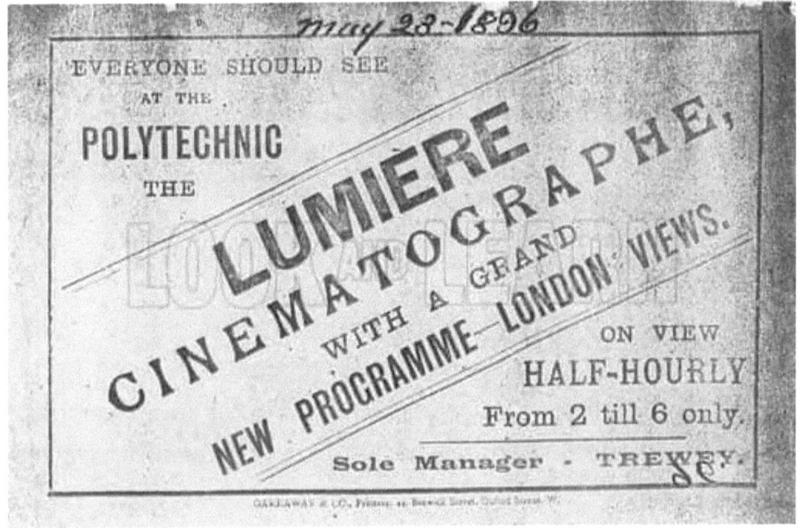

Ticket for the Lumiere Cinematographe in London (May 1896)

M. Lumiere's five-syllabled invention is yet in its infancy its possibilities are almost awe-inspiring. At present the photographs are no bigger than postage-stamps, and, thrown life-size on to the screen, they inevitably lose certain details. When practice has brought about perfection, where will the invention stop? Imagine it worked in connection with the phonograph. The past will become annihilated; our great Parliamentary debates, our monster meetings, our operatic and theatrical performances, will remain for ever, or even longer. I do not dare to think of the scientific and medical possibilities, but am content to dwell on the more popular ones. While the phonograph preserves the sounds, the Cin., &c., will do the rest. A trifle of about forty-five thousand exposures will preserve an Empire ballet intact for ever. Why did not M. Lumière arrange his invention before the exquisite Katrina became a thing of the past? Soon nothing that is beautiful will be mortal, and as the song has become immortal through the phonograph, the exquisite graces of the dance will be preserved by the new invention. Would not Horace have modified his famous ode to Postumus had he dreamt of such things as will soon be regarded as ordinary? I have for the last week been imagining some of the many things that will be represented or later. How splendidly a Spanish bull fight could be shown!

The present exhibition at the Empire Theatre, where, by the way, breathing-space is almost at a premium, is directed by M. Trewey, and I felt that I must call on him, in the interests of humanity at large, or rather, that large part of humanity given to *Sketch* reading.

I found M. Trewey on the stage of the Empire, smiling for all he is worth which is probably a large amount. No wonder he looked pleased. A few hours before he had been visited at the Polytechnic by the Duke and Duchess of Connaught, who had expressed their delight with his entertainment.

"M. Lumiere, of Lyons," he said, is my oldest friend, and he gave me the choice of the country in which I would show his invention. Of course, I chose England. I had intended to retire from work altogether, for" – and his eyes twinkled – "I have been a careful man But I thought this work would be very light, so I took it. Now, I never know a moment's rest, and I have promised the directors here to give at least one new picture every week. As soon as the fine weather sets in again," he went on, we shall do fresh work on the racecourse, river, and similar places. We are not going to be idle."

And, as though to prove his words, M. Trewey, with a hurried apology, bustled off to the centre of the stage with all the energy and enthusiasm of a very young man. I noticed that the machine was being rapidly prepared, and that one or two of the charming *corps de ballet* had evidently obtained permission to see the performance from the stage. Unfortunately for me, I was very much overdue at another house of entertainment. I could but sigh for the delight of the few occasions when my visits to Empire stageland have been longer. Then I departed.

Source: 'A Wonderful Invention: The Cinématographe of M. Lumière', *The Sketch*, 18 March 1896, p. 323

2

Living pictures

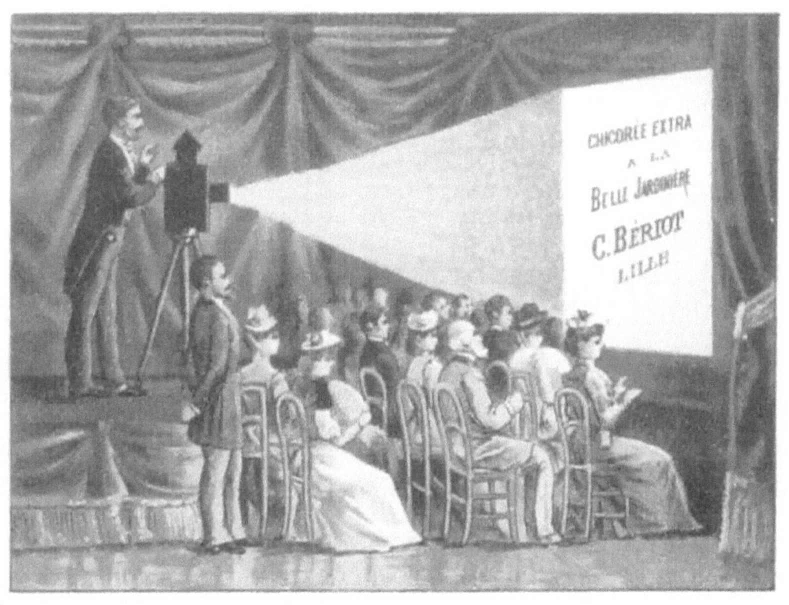

In presenting this book to my readers I feel the necessity of making a few remarks with regard to its scope. The subject of which it treats is, in earher years, so bound up with researches on Persistence of Vision that I have been sorely tempted to stray into many seductively interesting by paths. Limitations of time and space have, however, exercised a certain influence, and I have been compelled to restrict my work in absolute conformity with the title of my book. Therefore, none of the interesting apparatus for demonstrating persistence of vision find a place within these pages, nor have the various theories on the subject been discussed. I have somewhat reluctantly confined myself strictly to the description and history of apparatus for producing the illusion of motion. At the same time, my book (within its proper limits) commences early, and, at the conclusion of a review covering over two thousand years, will be found, I hope, fully " up to date." I have adopted the practice of italicising the name of each instrument when first met with in the Historical Section, and the Index will be found to include, in alphabetical order, not only names properly applied, but also such mis-spelled variations as I may have met with, and also many which have been erroneously used, they, like "the flowers which bloom in the spring" having "nothing to do with the case." The changes rung on Kine-, Cine-, and Vitaare so numerous — one might say irritating — that I am led to hope that the mathematical laws of permutation may break down, and, in defiance of arithmetical rules, thus create a necessity for radical changes in the naming of later machines. The descriptions in the list of British Patents must not be taken as full ; I see no necessity to reprint a mass of Government Blue-books which are available in full to the public, but I believe that every specification pertinent to my subject is at least mentioned, and I am convinced such a list is a necessary complement to an historical review. Furthermore, these patents will be found to include many ideas which may contain some useful germs, and although many of these crude conceptions have not been practically carried out, they at least afford food for thought. An acquaintance with the minuteness of the steps in the evolution of the Living Picture has caused me to attach value to even the slightest novelty, find it where I might. With regard to the Bibliography, I do not put it forward as exhaustive. Were it so, the valuable papers would be hidden among a number of reprints and comments. I merely append some of the more important references I have collected in the course of my reading, in order that others may pursue any point on which they desire further information than I have been able to supply in the space at my disposal. To this end the Index is especially directed ; I believe its utility will justify the labour I have expended upon it. In conclusion, I would say that my aim has been to express each fact as clearly as possible in a popular way, and to present in a connected form as much information as I could collect, in order that my book might not only provide a few hours pleasant reading, but also serve as a standard of reference on its subject. Finally, I should esteem it a favour if any reader who discovers an error, either of commission or omission, in my work would acquaint me with the fact, for "to err is human" ; and I should be pleased to find my critics approach the other extreme of the proverb cited.

***

source : Henry V. Hopwood, *Living pictures : their history, photo-production and practical working, with a digest of British patents and annotated bibliography*, London : Optician & Photographic Trades Review, 1899.

3

The psychology of theatre audiences

The drama is the only art, excepting oratory and certain forms of music, that is designed to appeal to a crowd instead of to an individual. The lyric poet writes for himself, and for such selected persons here and there throughout the world as may be wisely sympathetic enough to understand his musings. The essayist and the novelist write for a reader sitting alone in his library : whether ten such readers or a hundred thousand ultimately read a book, the w r riter speaks to each of them apart from all the others. It is the same with painting and with sculpture. Though a picture or a statue may be seen by a limitless succession of observers, its appeal is made always to the individual mind. But it is different with a play. Since a drama is, in essence, a story devised to be presented by actors on a stage before an audience, it must necessarily be designed to appeal at once to a multitude of people. We have to be alone in order to appreciate the Venus of Melos or the Sistine Madonna or the Ode to a Nightingale or the Egoist or the Religio Medici ; but who could sit alone in a wide theatre and see Cyrano de Bergerac performed? The sympathetic presence of a multitude of people would be as necessary to our appreciation of the play as solitude in all the other cases. And because the drama must be written for a crowd, it must be fashioned differently from the other, and less popular, forms of art.

No writer is really a dramatist unless he recognises this distinction of appeal; and if an author is not accustomed to writing for the crowd, he can hardly hope to make a satisfying play. Tennyson, the perfect poet ; Browning, the master of the human mind; Stevenson, the teller of enchantincrtales : — each of them failed when he tried to make a drama, because the conditions of his proper art had schooled him long in writing for the individual instead of for the crowd. A literary artist who writes for the individual may produce a great work of literature that is cast in the dramatic form; but the work will not be, in the practical sense, a play. Samson Agonistes, Faust, Pippa Passes, Peer Gynt, and the early dream-dramas of Maurice Maeterlinck, are something else than plays. They are not devised to be presented by actors on a stage before an audience. As a work of literature, A Blot in the ' Scutcheon is immeasurably greater than The Two Orphans; but as a play, it is immeasurably less. For even though, in this particular piece, Browning did try to write for the theatre (at the suggestion of Macready), he employed the same intricately intellectual method of character analysis that has made many of his poems the most solitude-compelling of modern literary works. Properly to appreciate his piece, you must be alone, just as you must be alone to read A Woman's Last Word. It is not written for a crowd; *The Two Orphans*, less weighty in wisdom, is. The second is a play.

La reine de Chypre, les acteurs et les spectateurs : [estampe] / par Marcelin [BNF]

The mightiest masters of the drama — Sophocles, Shakespeare, and Moliere — have recognised the popular character of its appeal and written frankly for the multitude. The crowd, therefore, has exercised a potent influence upon the dramatist in every era of the theatre. One person the lyric poet has to please, — himself ; to a single person only, or an unlimited succession of single persons, does the novelist address himself, and he may choose the sort of person he will write for; but the dramatist must always please the many. His themes, his thoughts, his emotions, are circumscribed by the limits of popular appreciation. He writes less freely than any other author; for he cannot pick his auditors. Mi. Henry James may, if he choose, write novels for the super-civilised ; but a crowd is never super-civilised, and therefore characters like those of Mr. James could never be successfully presented in the theatre. Treasure Island is a book for boys, both young and old; but a modem theatre crowd is composed largely of women, and the theme of such a story could scarcely be successful on the stage.

In order, therefore, to understand the limitations of the drama as an art, and clearly to define its scope, it is necessary to inquire into the psychology of theatre audiences. This subject presents two phases to the student. First, a theatre audience exhibits certain psychological traits that are common to all crowds, of whatever kind, — a political convention, the spectators at a ball-game, or a church congregation, for example. Second, it exhibits certain other traits which distinguish it from other kinds of crowds. These, in turn, will be considered in the present chapter. By the word crowd, as it is used in this discussion, is meant a multitude of people whose ideas and feelings have taken a set in a certain single direction, and who, because of this, exhibit a tendency to lose their individual self-consciousness in the general self-consciousness of the multitude. Any gathering of people for a specific purpose — whether of action or of worship or of amusement — tends to become, because of this purpose, a crowd, in the scientific sense. Now, a crowd has a mind of its own, apart from that of any of its individual members. The psychology of the crowd was little understood until late in the nineteenth century, when a great deal of attention was turned to it by a group of French philosophers.

The subject has been most fully studied by M. Gustave Le Bon, who devoted some two hundred pages to his *Psychologie des Foules* [1895]. According to M. Le Bon, a man, by the mere fact that he forms a factor of a crowd, tends to lose consciousness of those mental qualities in which he differs from his fellows, and becomes more keenly conscious than before of those other mental qualities in which he is at one with them. The mental qualities in which men differ from one another are the acquired qualities of intellect and character ; but the qualities in which they are at one are the innate basic passions of the race. A crowd, therefore, is less intellectual and more emotional than the individuals that compose it. It is less reasonable, less judicious, less disinterested, more credulous, more primitive, more partisan ; and hence, as M. Le Bon cleverly puts it, a man, by the mere fact that he forms a part of an organised crowd, is likely to descend several rungs on the ladder of civilisation. Even the most cultured and intellectual of men, when he forms an atom of a crowd, tends to lose consciousness of his acquired mental qualities and to revert to his primal simplicity and sensitiveness of mind.

The dramatist, therefore, because he writes for a crowd, writes for a comparatively uncivilised and uncultivated mind, a mind richly human, vehement in approbation, emphatic in disapproval, easily credulous, eagerly enthusiastic, boyishly heroic, and somewhat carelessly unthinking. Now, it has been found in practice that the only thing that will keenly interest a crowd is a struggle of some sort or other. Speaking empirically, the late Ferdinand Brunetiere, in 1893, stated that the drama has dealt always with a struggle between human wills; and his statement, formulated in the catchphrase, “No struggle, no drama”, has since become a commonplace of dramatic criticism. But, so far as I know, no one has yet realised the main reason for this, which is, simply, that characters are interesting to a crowd only in those crises of emotion that bring them to the grapple. A single individual, like the reader of an essay or a novel, may be interested intellectually in those gentle influences beneath which a character unfolds itself as mildly as a water-lily; but to what Thackeray called “that savage child, the crowd,” a character does not appeal except in moments of contention. There never yet has been a time when the theatre could compete successfully against the amphitheatre. Plautus and Terence complained that the Roman public preferred a gladiatorial combat to their plays ; a bear-baiting or a cockfight used to empty Shakespeare’s theatre on the Bankside; and there is not a matinee in town to-day that can hold its own against a foot-ball game. Forty thousand people gather annually from all quarters of the East to see Yale and Harvard meet upon the field, while such a crowd could not be aggregated from New York alone to see the greatest play the world has yet produced. For the crowd demands a fight ; and where the actual exists, it will scarcely be contented with the semblance.

Hence the drama, to interest at all, must cater to this longing for contention, which is one of the primordial instincts of the crowd. It must present its characters in some struggle of the wills, whether it be flippant, as in the case of Benedick and Beatrice; or delicate, as in that of Viola and Orsino; or terrible, with *Macbeth*; or piteous, with *Lear*. The crowd is more partisan than the individual; and therefore, in following this struggle of the drama, it desires always to take sides. There is no fun in seeing a foot-ball game unless you care about who wins ; and there is very little fun in seeing a play unless the dramatist allows you to throw your sympathies on one side or the other of the struggle. Hence, although in actual life both parties to a conflict are often partly right and partly wrong, and it is hard to choose between them, the dramatist usually simplifies the struggle in his plays by throwing the balance of right strongly on one side. Hence, from the ethical standpoint, the simplicity of theatre characters.

Desdemona is all innocence, Iago all deviltry. Hence also the conventional heroes and villains of melodrama, — these to be hissed and those to be applauded. Since the crowd is comparatively lacking in the judicial faculty and cannot look upon a play from a detached and disinterested point of view, it is either all for or all against a character; and in either case its judgment is frequently in defiance of the rules of reason. It will hear no word against Camille, though an individual would judge her to be wrong, and it has no sympathy with Pere Duval. It idolizes Raffles, who is a liar and a thief ; it shuts its ears to Marion Allardyce, the defender of virtue in Letty. It wants its sympathetic characters, to love ; its antipathetic characters, to hate ; and it hates and loves them as unreasonably as a savage or a child. The trouble with Hedda Gabler as a play is that it contains not a single personage that the audience can love.

Les Spectateurs applaudissant

BNF (Observations théâtrales, n° 8), 1831

The crowd demands those so-called "sympathetic" parts that every actor, for this reason, longs to represent. And since the crowd is partisan, it wants its favored characters to win. Hence the convention of the "happy ending", insisted on by managers who feel the pulse of the public. The blind Louise, in *The Two Orphans*, will get her sight back, never fear. Even the wicked Oliver, in *As You Like It*, must turn over a new leaf and marry a pretty girl.

Next to this prime instinct of partisanship in watching a contention, one of the most important traits in the psychology of crowds is their extreme credulity. A crowd will nearly always believe anything that it sees and almost anything that it is told. An audience composed entirely of individuals who have no belief in ghosts will yet accept the *Ghost in Hamlet* as a fact. Bless you, they have seen him ! The crowd accepts the disguise of Rosalind, and never wonders why Orlando does not recognise his love. To this extreme credulity of the crowd is due the long line of plays that are founded on mistaken identity, — farces like *The Comedy of Errors* and melodramas like *The Lyons Mail*, for example. The crowd, too, will accept without demur any condition precedent to the story of a play, however impossible it might seem to the mind of the individual. *Oedipus King* has been married to his mother many years before the play begins; but the Greek crowd forbore to ask why, in so long a period, the enormity had never been discovered. The central situation of *She Stoops to Conquer* seems impossible to the individual mind, but is eagerly accepted by the crowd. Individual critics find fault with Thomas Heywood's lovely old play, *A Woman Killed with Kindness*, on the ground that though Frankford's noble forgiveness of his erring wife is beautiful to contemplate, Mrs. Frankford's infidelity is not sufficiently motivated, and the whole story, therefore, is untrue. But Heywood, writing for the crowd, said frankly, "If you will grant that Mrs. Frankford was unfaithful, I can tell you a lovely story about her husband, who was a gentleman worth knowing: otherwise there can't be any story" ; and the Elizabethan crowd, eager for the story, was willing to oblige the dramatist with the necessary credulity.

There is this to be said about the credulity of an audience, however, — that it will believe what it sees much more readily than what it hears. It might not believe in the ghost of Hamlet's father if the ghost were merely spoken of and did not walk upon the stage. If a dramatist would convince his audience of the generosity or the treachery of one character or another, he should not waste words either praising or blaming the character, but should present him to the eye in the perormance of a generous or treacherous action.

The audience hears wise w y ords from *Polonius* when he gives his parting admonition to his son ; but the same audience sees him made a fool of by *Prince Hamlet*, and will not think him wise. The fact that a crowd's eyes are more keenly receptive than its ears is the psychologic basis for the maxim that in the theatre action speaks louder than words. It also affords a reason why plays of which the audience does not understand a single word are frequently successful. Mme. Sarah Bernhardt's thrilling performance of *La Tosca* has always aroused enthusiasm in London and New-York, where the crowd, as a crowd, could not understand the language of the play.

Les Spectateurs pleurant

(Observations théâtrales n°3) Oeuvre de Cl. Pruche, 1837 [BNF]

Another primal characteristic of the mind of the crowd is its susceptibility to emotional contagion. A cultivated individual reading *The School for Scandal* at home alone will be intelligently appreciative of its delicious humor; but it is difficult to imagine him laughing over it aloud. Yet the same individual, when submerged in a theatre crowd, will laugh heartily over this very play, largely because other people near him are laughing too. Laughter, tears, enthusiasm, all the basic human emotions, thrill and tremble through an audience, because each member of the crowd feels that he is surrounded by other people who are experiencing the same emotion as his own. In the sad part of a play it is hard to keep from weeping if the woman next to you is wiping her eyes; and still harder is it to keep from laughing, even at a sorry jest, if the man on the other side is roaring in vociferous cachinnation. Successful dramatists play upon the susceptibility of a crowd by serving up raw morsels of crude humor and pathos for the unthinking to wheeze and blubber over, knowing that these members of the audience will excite their more phlegmatic neighbors by contagion. The practical dictum that every laugh in the first act is worth money in the box-office is founded on this psychologic truth. Even puns as bad as Mr. Zangwill's are of value early in a play to set on some quantity of barren spectators and get the house accustomed to a titter. Scenes like the football episodes in *The College Widow and Strongheart*, or the battle in *The Round Up*, are nearly always sure to raise the roof ; for it is usually sufficient to set everybody on the stage a-cheering in order to make the audience cheer too by sheer contagion. Another and more classical example was the speechless triumph of *Henry V*'s return victorious, in Richard Mansfield's sumptuous production of the play. Here the audience felt that he was every inch a king ; for it had caught the fervor of the crowd upon the stage.

This same emotional contagion is, of course, the psychologic basis for the French system of the claque, or band of hired applauders seated in the centre of the house. The leader of the claque knows his cues as if he were an actor in the piece, and at the psychologic moment the claqueurs burst forth with their clatter and start the house applauding. Applause begets applause in the theatre, as laughter begets laughter and tears beget tears. But not only is the crowd more emotional than the individual ; it is also more sensuous. It has the lust of the eye and of the ear, — the savage's love of gaudy color, the child's love of soothing sound.

It is fond of flaring flags and blaring trumpets. Hence the rich-costumed processions of the Elizabethan stage, many years before the use of scenery ; and hence, in our own day, the success of pieces like *The Darling of the Gods* and *The Rose of the Rancho*. Color, light, and music, artistically blended, will hold the crowd better than the most absorbing story. This is the reason for the vogue of musical comedy, with its pretty girls, and gaudy shifts of scenery and lights, and tricksy, tripping melodies and dances.

Both in its sentiments and in its opinions, the crowd is comfortably commonplace. It is, as a crowd, incapable of original thought and of any but inherited emotion. It has no speculation in its eyes. What it feels was felt before the flood; and what it thinks, its fathers thought before it. The most effective moments in the theatre are those that appeal to basic and commonplace emotions, — love of woman, love of home, love of country, love of right, anger, jealousy, revenge, ambition, lust, and treachery. So great for centuries has been the inherited influence of the Christian religion that any adequate play whose motive is self-sacrifice is almost certain to succeed. Even when the self-sacrifice is unwise and ignoble, as in the first act of *Frou-Frou*, the crowd will give it vehement approval. Countless plays have been made upon the man who unselfisnly assumes responsibility for another's guilt. The great tragedies have familiar themes, — ambition in *Macbeth*, jealousy in *Othello*, filial ingratitude in *Lear*; there is nothing in these motives that the most unthinking audience could fail to understand. No crowd can resist the fervor of a patriot who goes down scornful before many spears. Show the audience a flag to die for, or a stalking ghost to be avenged, or a shred of honor to maintain against agonizing odds, and it will thrill with an enthusiasm as ancient as the human race. Few are the plays that can succeed without the moving force of love, the most familiar of all emotions. These themes do not require that the audience shall think.

But for the speculative, the original, the new, the crowd evinces little favor. If the dramatist holds ideas of religion, or of politics, or of social law, that are in advance of his time, he must keep them to himself or else his plays will fail. Nimble wits, like Mr. Shaw, who scorn tradition, can attain a popular success only through the crowd's inherent love of fads; they cannot long succeed when they run counter to inherited ideas. The great successful dramatists, like Moliere and Shakespeare, have always thought with the crowd on all essential questions. Their views of religion, of morality, of politics, of law, have been the views of the populace, nothing more. They never raise questions that cannot quickly be answered by the crowd, through the instinct of inherited experience. No mind was ever, in the philosophic sense, more commonplace than that of Shakespeare. He had no new ideas. He was never radical, and seldom even progressive. He was a careful money-making business man, fond of food and drink and out-of-doors and laughter, a patriot, a lover, and a gentleman. Greatly did he know things about people; greatly, also, could he write. But he accepted the religion, the politics, and the social ethics of his time, without ever bothering to wonder if these things might be improved.

The great speculative spirits of the world, those who overturn tradition and discover new ideas, have had minds far different from this. They have not written plays. It is to these men, — the philosopher, the essayist, the novelist, the lyric poet, — that each of us turns for what is new in thought. But from the dramatist the crowd desires only the old, old thought. It has no patience for consideration ; it will listen only to what it knows already. If, therefore, a great man has a new doctrine to expound, let him set it forth in a book of essays; or, if he needs must sugar-coat it with a story, let him expound it in a novel, whose appeal will be to the individual mind. Not until a doctrine is old enough to have become generally accepted is it ripe for exploitation in the theatre.

This point is admirably illustrated by two of the best and most successful plays of recent seasons. The Witching Hour, by Mr. Augustus Thomas, and The Servant in the House, by Mr. Charles Rann Kennedy, were both praised by many critics for their " novelty " ; but to me one of the most significant and instructive facts about them is that neither of them was, in any real respect, novel in the least. Consider for a moment the deliberate and careful lack of novelty in the ideas which Mr. Thomas so skilfully set forth. What Mr. Thomas really did was to gather and arrange as many as possible of the popularly current thoughts concerning telepathy and cognate subjects, and to tell the public what they themselves had been wondering about and thinking during the last few years. The timeliness of the play lay in the fact that it was produced late enough in the history of its subject to be selectively resumptive, and not nearly so much in the fact that it was produced early enough to forestall other dramatic presentations of the same materials. Mr. Thomas has himself explained, in certain semi-public conversations, that he postponed the composition of this play — on which his mind had been set for many years — until the general public had become sufficiently accustomed to the ideas which he intended to set forth. Ten years before, this play would have been novel, and would undoubtedly have failed. When it was produced, it was not novel, but resumptive, in its thought; and therefore it succeeded. For one of the surest ways of succeeding in the theatre is to sum up and present dramatically all that the crowd has been thinking for some time concerning any subject of importance. The dramatist should be the catholic collector and wise interpreter of those ideas which the crowd, in its conservatism, feels already to be safely true.

And if T*he Servant in the House* will — as I believe — outlive *The Witching Hour*, it will be mainly because, in the author's theme and his ideas, it is older by many, many centuries. The theme of Mr. Thomas's play — namely, that thought is in itself a dynamic force and has the virtue and to some extent the power of action — is, as I have just explained, not novel, but is at least recent in the history of thinking. It is a theme which dates itself as belonging to the present generation, and is likely to lose interest for the next. But Mr. Kennedy's theme — namely, that when discordant human beings ascend to meet each other in the spirit of brotherly love, it may truly be said that God is resident among them — is at least as old as the gentle-hearted Galilean, and, being dateless, belongs to future generations as well as to the present. Mr. Thomas has been skilfully resumptive of a passing period of popular thought ; but Mr. Kennedy has been resumptive on a larger scale, and has built his play upon the wisdom of the centuries. Paradoxical as it may seem, the very reason why The Servant in the House struck so many critics as being strange and new is that, in its thesis and its thought, it is as old as the world.

The truth of this point seems to me indisputable. I know that the best European playwrights of the present day are striving to use the drama as a vehicle for the expression of advanced ideas, especially in regard to social ethics ; but in doing this, I think, they are mistaking the scope of the theatre. They are striving to say in the drama what might be said better in the essay or the novel. As the exposition of a theory, Mr. Shaw's Man and Superman is not nearly so effective as the writings of Schopenhauer and Nietzsche, from whom the playwright borrowed his ideas. The greatest works of Ibsen can be appreciated only by the cultured individual and not by the uncultured crowd. That is why the breadth of his appeal will never equal that of Shakespeare, in spite of his unfathomable intellect and his perfect mastery of the technique of his art. Only his more commonplace plays — A Doll's House, for example — have attained a wide success. And a wide success is a thing to be desired for other than material reasons. Surely it is a good thing for the public that Hamlet never fails.

Orange, Théâtre Antique, la scène et les spectateurs : représentation par la Comédie Française "Les Funérailles d'Homère" [BNF, Département des Arts du Spectacle, Fonds Rondel] 1906.

The conservatism of the greatest dramatists asserts itself not only in their thoughts but even in the mere form of their plays. It is the lesser men who invent new tricks of technique and startle the public with innovations. Moliere merely perfected the type of Italian comedy that his public long had known. Shakespeare quietly adopted the forms that lesser men had made the crowd familiar with. He imitated Lyly in *Love's Labour's Lost*, Greene in *As You Like It*, Marlowe in *Richard III*, Kyd in *Hamlet*, and Fletcher in *The Tempest*. He did the old thing better than the other men had done it, — that is all.

Yet this is greatly to Shakespeare's credit. He was wise enough to feel that what the crowd wanted, both in matter and in form, was what was needed in the greatest drama. In saying that Shakespeare's mind was commonplace, I meant to tender him the highest praise. In his commonplaceness lies his sanity. He is so greatly usual that he can understand all men and sympathise with them. He is above novelty. His wisdom is greater than the wisdom of the few; he is the heir of all the ages, and draws his wisdom from the general mind of man. And it is largely because of this that he represents ever the ideal of the dramatist. He who would write for the theatre must not despise the crowd.

All of the above-mentioned characteristics of theatre audiences, their instinct for contention and for partisanship, their credulity, their sensuousness, their susceptibility to emotional contagion, their incapacity for original thought, their conservatism, and their love of the commonplace, appear in every sort of crowd, as M. Le Bon has proved with ample illustration. It remains for us to notice certain traits in which theatre audiences differ from other kinds of crowds.

In the first place, a theatre audience is composed of individuals more heterogeneous than those that make up a political, or social, or sporting, or religious convocation. The crowd at a foot-ball game, at a church, at a social or political convention, is by its very purpose selective of its elements : it is made up entirely of college-folk, or Presbyterians, or Prohibitionists, or Republicans, as the case may be. But a theatre audience is composed of all sorts and conditions of men. The same theatre in New York contains the rich and the poor, the literate and the illiterate, the old and the young, the native and the naturalised. The same play, therefore, must appeal to all of these. It follows that the dramatist must be broader in his appeal than any other artist. He cannot confine his message to any single caste of society. In the same single work of art he must incorporate elements that will interest all classes of humankind.

Those promising dramatic movements that have confined their appeal to a certain single stratum of society have failed ever, because of this, to achieve the highest excellence. The trouble with Roman comedy is that it was written for an audience composed chiefly of freedmen and slaves. The patrician caste of Rome walked wide of the theatres. Only the dregs of society gathered to applaud the comedies of Plautus and Terence. Hence the oversimplicity of their prologues, and their tedious reptition cf the obvious. Hence, also, their vulgarity, their horse-play, their obscenity. Here was fine dramatic genius led astray, because the time was out of joint. Similarly, the trouble with French tragedy, in the classicist period of Corneille and Racine, is that it was written only for the finest caste of society, — the patrician coterie of a patrician cardinal. Hence its over-niceness, and

its appeal to the ear rather than to the eye. Terence aimed too low and Racine aimed too high. Each of them, therefore, shot wide of the mark; while Moliere, who wrote at once for patrician and lebeian, scored a hit.

The really great dramatic movements of the world — that of Spain in the age of Calderon and Lope, that of England in the spacious times of great Elizabeth, that of France from 1830 to the present hour — have broadened their appeal to every class. The queen and the orange-girl joyed together in the healthiness of Rosalind; the king and the gamin laughed together at the rogueries of Scapin. The breadth of Shakespeare's appeal remains one of the most significant facts in the history of the drama. Tell a filthy-faced urchin of the gutter that you know about a play that shows a ghost that stalks and talks at midnight underneath a castle-tower, and a man that makes believe he is out of his head so that he can get the

better of a wicked king, and a girl that goes mad and drowns herself, and a play within the play, and a funeral in a churchyard, and a duel with poisoned swords, and a great scene at the end in which nearly every one gets killed: tell him this, and watch his eyes gi'ow wide! I have been to a thirty-cent performance of *Othello* in a middlewestern town, and have felt the audience thrill with the headlong hurry of the action. Yet these are the plays that cloistered students study for their wisdom and their style! And let us not forget, in this connection, that a similar breadth of appeal is neither necessary nor greatly to be desired in those forms of literature that, unlike the drama, are not written for the crowd. The greatest non-dramatic poet and the greatest novelist in English are appreciated only by the few ; but this is not in the least to the discredit of Milton and of Meredith. One indication of the greatness of Mr. Kipling's story, They, is that very few have learned to read it.

Victor Hugo, in his preface to *Ruy Bias*, has discussed this entire principle from a slightly different point of view. He divides the theatre audience into three classes — the thinkers, who demand characterisation; the women, who demand passion ; and the mob, who demand action and insists that every great play must appeal to all three classes at once. Certainly Ruy Bias itself fulfils this desideratum, and is great in the breadth of its appeal. Yet although all three of the necessary elements appear in the play, it has more action than passion and more passion than characterisation. And this fact leads us to the theory, omitted by Victor Hugo from his preface, that the mob is more important than the women and the women more important than the thinkers, in the average theatre audience. Indeed, a deeper consideration of the subject almost leads us to discard the thinkers as a psychologic force and to obliterate the distinction between the women and the mob. It is to an unthinking and feminine-minded mob that the dramatist must first of all appeal; and this leads us to believe that action with passion for its motive is the prime essential for a play.

Fichot, Charles (1817-1904), L'incendie de l'Opéra-Comique. La panique. Sortie des spectateurs affolés. 1887.
Bibliothèque-musée de l'Opéra.
[BNF, Département des Arts du Spectacle]

For, nowadays at least, it is most essential that the drama should appeal to a crowd of women. Practically speaking, our matinee audiences are composed entirely of women, and our evening audiences are composed chiefly of women and the men that they have brought with them. Very few men go to the theatre unattached; and these few are not important enough, from the theoretic standpoint, to alter the psychologic aspect of the audience. And it is this that constitutes one of the most important differences between a modem theatre audience and other kinds of crowds.

The influence of this fact upon the dramatist is very potent. First of all, as I have said, it forces him to deal chiefly in action with passion for its motive. And this necessity accounts for the preponderance of female characters over male in the large majority of the greatest modern plays. Notice Nora Helmer, Mrs. Alving, Hedda Gabler; notice Magda and Camille; notice Mrs. Tanqueray, Mrs. Ebbsmith, Iris, and Letty, — to cite only a few examples. Furthermore, since women are by nature comparatively inattentive, the femininity of the modem theatre audience forces the dramatist to employ the elementary technical tricks of repetition and parallelism, in order to keep his play clear, though much of it be unattended to. Eugene Scribe, who knew the theatre, used to say that every important statement in the exposition of a play must be made at least three times. This, of course, is seldom necessary in a novel, where things may be said once for all.

The prevailing inattentiveness of a theatre audience at the present day is due also to the fact that it is peculiarly conscious of itself, apart from the play that it has come to see. Many people " go to the theatre," as the phrase is, without caring much whether they see one play or another; what they want chiefly is to immerse themselves in a theatre audience. This is especially true, in New York, of the large percentage of people from out of town who " go to the theatre " merely as one phase of their metropolitan experience. It is true, also, of the many women in the boxes and the orchestra who go less to see than to be seen. It is one of the great difficulties of the dramatist that he must capture and enchain the attention of an audience thus composed. A man does not pick up a novel unless he cares to read it; but many people go to the theatre chiefly for the sense of being there. Certainly, therefore, the problem of the dramatist is, in this respect, more difficult than that of the novelist, for he must make his audience lose consciousness of itself in the consciousness of his play.

One of the most essential differences between a theatre audience and other kinds of crowds lies in the purpose for which it is convened. This purpose is always recreation. A theatre audience is therefore less serious than a church congregation or a political or social convention. It does not come to be edified or educated; it has no desire to be taught: what it wants is to have its emotions played upon. It seeks amusement — in the widest sense of the word — amusement through laughter, sympathy, terror, and tears. And it is amusement of this sort that the great dramatists have ever given it.

The trouble with most of the dreamers who league themselves for the uplifting of the stage is that they consider the theatre with an illogical solemnity. They base their efforts on the proposition that a theatre audience ought to w'ant to be edified. As a matter of fact, no audience ever does. Moliere and Shakespeare, who knew the limits of their art, never said a word about uplifting the stage. They wrote plays to please the crowd ; and if, through their inherent greatness, they became teachers as well as entertainers, they did so without any tall talk about the solemnity of their mission. Their audiences learned largely, but they did so unawares, — God being with them when they knew it not. The demand for an endowed theatre in America comes chiefly from those who believe that a great play cannot earn its own living. Yet Hamlet has made more money than any other play in English; *The School for Scandal* never fails to draw ; and in our own day we have seen *Cyrano de Bergerac* coining money all around the world.

There were not any endowed theatres in Elizabethan London. Give the crowd the sort of plays it wants, and you will not have to seek beneficence to keep your theatre floating. But, on the other hand, no endowed theatre will ever lure the crowd to listen to the sort of plays it does not want. There is a wise maxim appended to one of Mr. George Ade's Fables in Slang: "In uplifting, get underneath". If the theatre in America is weak, what it needs is not endowment: it needs great and popular plays. Why should we waste our money and our energy trying to make the crowd come to see *The Master Builder*, or *A Blot in the 'Scutcheon*, or *The Hour Glass*, or *Pelleas and Melisande*?

It is willing enough to come without urging to see Othello and *The Second Mrs. Tanqueray*. Give us one great dramatist who understands the crowd, and we shall not have to form societies to propagate his art. Let us cease our prattle of the theatre for the few. Any play that is really great as drama will interest the many.

One point remains to be considered. In any theatre audience there are certain individuals who do not belong to the crowd. They are in it, but not of it; for they fail to merge their individual self-consciousness in the general self-consciousness of the multitude. Such are the professional critics, and other confirmed frequenters of the theatre. It is not for them primarily that plays are written; and any one who has grown individualised through the theatre-going habit cannot help looking back regretfully upon those fresher days when he belonged, unthinking, to the crowd. A first-night audience is anomalous, in that it is composed largely of individuals opposed to self-surrender; and for this reason, a first-night judgment of the merits of a play is rarely final. The dramatist has written for a crowd, and he is judged by individuals. Most dramatic critics will tell you that they long to lose themselves in the crowd, and regret the aloofness from the play that comes of their profession. It is because of this aloofness of the critic that most dramatic criticism fails.

Throughout the present discussion, I have insisted on the point that the great dramatists have always written primarily for the many. Yet now I must add that when once they have fulfilled this prime necessity, they may also write secondarily for the few. And the very greatest have always done so. In so far as he was a dramatist, Shakespeare wrote for the crowd ; in so far as he was a lyric poet, he wrote for himself ; and in so far as he was a sage and a stylist, he wrote for the individual. In making sure of his appeal to the many, he earned the right to appeal to the few. At the thirty-cent performance of Othello that I spoke of, I was probably the only person present who failed to submerge his individuality beneath the common consciousness of the audience. Shakespeare made a play that could appeal to the rabble of that middle-western town ; but he wrote it in a verse that none of them could hear :

— Not poppy, nor mandragora,

Nor all the drowsy syrups of the world,

Shall ever medicine thee to that sweet sleep

Which thou ow'dst yesterday.

The greatest dramatist of all, in writing for the crowd, did not neglect the individual.

***

Source : "The Psychology of Theatre audicences", in *The theory of the theatre, and other principles of dramatic criticism* (1910) by Clayton Meeker Hamilton (1881-1946), New York, H. Holt and company, 1910, pp. 30-58. Public Domain.

4

Movies as an educational force

MOTION-PHOTOGRAPHY AS AN EDUCATIONAL FORCE

There remains no doubt whatever that the cinematograph has completely won over the great public — the many millions who are constantly seeking fresh fields of amusement and diversion. Of all the classes that patronise the moving-picture entertainment, the children form the one most open to its influence and most responsive to what it offers them ; and it is this well-known impressionableness of the young mind that has set people thinking of the educational responsibility of the moving-picture show. From this it is but a step to the question, May not the cinematograph be brought into the school room?

The subject has several aspects that are worth treating somewhat at length. The firm of Pathé Frères has here, as in so many other directions, been first in the field. Let us examine some of its educational films.

The peculiar properties possessed by the magnet are profoundly mysterious to the child. Textbooks may be written in the simplest language and freely illustrated with diagrams, but the points still remain somewhat obscure. This French manufacturing company has prepared a film, "The Magnet," in which the well-known subject-matter of the school book is illustrated, and the phenomena described therein are demonstrated in a simple manner by visual records of the peculiar properties possessed by the magnet.

The familiar experiments with the magnet and iron filings are treated simply and with endless variety. If the pupils see the teacher perform the manipulations with filings and magnet in the usual way, the experiment conveys no tangible idea, and interest is not greatly aroused. But when the same magnet is thrown upon the screen in movement, and is ten feet or so in height, while the iron filings are so magnified that they resemble not dust, but thorns or long pins, a more convincing and indelible impression is conveyed.

One may have seen many diagrams showing the lines of force, as they are called. But no diagram can produce the unforgettable impression gained by the sight of the phenomenon itself occurring before the eyes. The iron filings may be seen resolving themselves into the two distinct groups about the poles, as if imbued with life, and the process may be followed from beginning to end with perfect ease, owing to the size to which the filings are magnified in projection.

The operation of natural laws is indelibly impressed upon the schoolboy when he is shown some novel experiment in physics carried out upon the screen. Physiology and anatomy can be taught by producing pictures taken by X-ray photography.

History ought surely to be a successful field for the educational cinematograph. The portrayal by Pathé Frères of episodes during the Reign of Terror and the Napoleonic era ; the representation of the Normans landing in England, the discovery of America by Columbus — these and similar pictures have already shown the wide possibilities of the historical film. Of course, great care must be taken to adhere to strict historical truth in fact and setting; when they will greatly serve to fix in the pupil's mind events, and historical atmosphere, and aid him in distinguishing various periods.

The fact that this film is produced in natural colours enhances its effect; a schoolboy would be hard indeed to impress if he failed to appreciate the wonderful significance of this evolution of the hyacinth from the bulb to the flowering stage. Again, he is enabled to witness upon the screen the birth of the common housefly, and its entire span of existence. He can see how ants work and live, and how the bee manufactures its honey. As a corollary to the matter-of-fact and uninteresting textbook the cinematograph film cannot be excelled. It presents in actual movement what mere words, which have to be" committed to memory, seek to convey without any durable result. Indeed, there is not the slightest doubt that a thousand pictures will impress themselves upon the school boy's mind, and impart to him more definite knowledge of their subject in one minute than hours of hammering with the aid of text-book and blackboard. Even actual ocular demonstration fails to be so convincing as a projection upon a whitened sheet, where everything immediately concerned is magnified to an extreme degree.

The inventor of the Kinetoscope, Mr. Thomas Edison, is of opinion that the cinematograph will displace all other methods in the schoolroom for the teaching of geography. Both teachers and pupils will be inclined to agree with this dictum. A teacher may talk for hours about the tremendous height of the peaks in the Andes, the racial characteristics of the natives of Abyssinia, or the manner in which rivers are born on the flanks of mighty glaciers. But words sometimes convey very little to the immature mind. Throw upon the screen a series of pictures of an actual journey, and the youngster gleans the facts without the slightest effort. He sees the towering, snowcapped rocks with their precipitous flanks ; the melting snow and ice flowing down from the mighty glacier and forming a tempestuous, rushing river; he sees in their natural surroundings the folk of a hundred strange and distant tribes. Perhaps he is transported for the time to the deck of a steamer driving its way up through the St, Lawrence River and the Great Lakes. Books and pictures have given him but a faint idea of these noble waters ; but when he sees their beauty, and witnesses the enormous traffic carried upon their broad bosoms, figures and facts take on new significance, and are never forgotten.

Whatever scene he sees, from the Atlantic to the Pacific, from the Arctic to the Antarctic circle, that scene becomes henceforth not a mere spot on the map, but a living reality.

One of the most remarkable series of pictures worthy of inclusion in this category is that obtained of Mount Etna in eruption. The cinematograph operator displayed wonderful daring in venturing to the verge. of the crater of this vent to internal fires. The reward for his intrepidity certainly conveys a more realistic and vivid impression of a belching volcano than the most imaginative flights of description in textbooks.

The success of the educational campaign of the cinematograph depends upon the suitability of the film. The cinematographer has roved through all the fields of science securing interesting pictures in metallurgy, natural history, manufacturing industries, electricity, agriculture, horticulture, and so forth. The educational value of the films now produced is beyond dispute ; but it may be that they are somewhat too old for children. The film manufacturers have, up to the present, chiefly consulted the tastes of adults; and the films of a distinctly educational character which they produce appeal to the mature rather than to the child mind. On the other hand, it should not be at all difficult to produce films which, like the one already described, representing experiments with the magnet, would give regular instead of incidental instruction upon subjects actually treated in schools — animated textbooks, in short. But as yet the picture producer has not received sufficient encouragement from the educational authorities to warrant him in preparing such films.

Unfortunately, the feeling against the moving picture has not been entirely eliminated, despite its tremendous popularity. Once an energetic Board of Education realises the possibilities of cinematography as a supplement to the information conveyed by textbooks and manuals, the film manufacturers will hasten to supply the demand thus created. The last obstacle will have been removed; for the field presents no special mechanical difficulties, the only serious one having been removed by the discovery of the non-inflammable film. The perfecting of this film has obviated the necessity of confining the installation within an iron box — a requirement which militated very appreciably against the introduction of the cinematograph into schools.

A striking illustration of the educational value of moving pictures is revealed in the beautiful series of "Empire" pictures which are being secured by Messrs. William Butcher and Sons. They are completing what may be described best as a cinematographic encyclopsedia of Greater Britain — its peoples, resources, industries, sports, and scenic beauties. Every corner of the Empire is being searched for entrancing pictorial contributions to this project.

As might have been expected, others beside educational institutions have seen in the moving-picture show a powerful instrument of propaganda. Political, charitable, municipal, and numerous other organisations have pressed the celluloid ribbon into service to aid them in their crusades. It has been of far-reaching utility in preaching the gospel of sanitation and prosecuting the war against disease, for the films convey their lessons in a terribly realistic manner. The Americans have produced a striking film for the dissemination of information as to how to combat advantageously the ravages of the great "White Plague" of consumption. The various American hygiene associations also have pressed home their campaign against the common housefly with commendable vigour by means of the cinematograph. Other photographs of a similar character have been produced in various places for the purpose of initiating the public into the causes of certain diseases and maladies, and the best means of prevention or treatment.

Medical science has profitted materially from the perfection of the art and its application to surgery. It is not always possible for students to be present at a peculiarly delicate and abnormal operation. Although the subject may be described at length in the technical papers, words fail to be so emphatic as a pictorial reproduction of the feat. Not only can the operation be followed closely when reproduced upon the screen, but, if desired, any particular phase in the achievement can be selected, and by enlargement upon photographic paper it can be subjected to closer and more minute investigation at leisure.

Even the Government has not failed to recognise the power of the cinematograph. Some years ago Mr. Robert Paul applied to the War Office for permission to film scenes in a soldier's life. The facilities were granted, and some first-class pictures were obtained. They proved immensely popular with the public, and were far more potent as a means of inducing enlistment with the colours than the most glowing word-pictures painted by glib, persuasive recruiting sergeants. This idea has been copied by other nations, and today the cinematograph is regarded as an indispensable weapon for attracting recruits to the land and sea services.

Religious institutions have not been backward in realising the value of animated pictures in preaching the gospel of faith. The producer, by means of the stage and actors, can present any episode from the Creation to the Resurrection. The world before the Deluge, the toil of the Israelites in the land of the Pharaohs, the Sacrifice of Abraham, the Passage of the Red Sea, with the destruction of the Egyptian hosts, the story of Samson and Delilah, the Fall of Babylon, scenes from the Life of Christ all these and many others help to familiarise both old and young with the Bible stories, and add wonderfully to their convincingness, as the following episode shows :' — A teacher was describing the Passage of the Red Sea. The children followed his words intently ; and his peroration was accompanied by a piping voice exclaiming :

" Yes, teacher, I know that is right "

" Why ? " asked the somewhat startled teacher.

" Because I saw it I "

The teacher was perhaps prepared to chide at this flight of imagination ; but the child soon explained that the previous evening she had been to a picture theatre and had seen the Israelites crossing the Red Sea.

Among the American preachers the significance of the cinematograph is beginning to be recognised. Ministers see in the projector a valuable adjunct to their teaching, and are disposed to introduce it into their churches. I am at liberty to quote in this connection a letter from one of the leading luminaries in American church circles, which was received by Mr. Richard G. Hollaman. The divine wrote : "My opinion is that the moving picture is the coming great educator. This I believe to be true, not only in the education of the youth, but in the church. I believe in a very few years every well-equipped church will have a moving-picture apparatus, so that the minister will appeal to the eye more than to the ear."

Poster from 1896 advertising the Cinématographe Lumière, with the heterogeneous audience watching *L'Arroseur Arrosé* [public domain]

***

source : Frederick A Talbot, *Moving pictures : how they are made and worked*. Philadelphia : J.B. Lippincott Co., 1912.

5

Writing the Photoplay

4. Where to Look for Titles

Good titles are everywhere—if you know how to find them. The Bible, Shakespeare, all the poets, books and plays that you read, newspapers, even advertisements on billboards and in street cars, all contain either suggestions for titles or complete titles, waiting only to be picked out and used. But be sure that someone else has not forestalled you!

Sayings, proverbs, and well-known quotations are a fruitful source of titles, as we have already intimated. But sometimes the real significance and value of such a title are not apparent to a great many of the spec[Pg 81]tators until they have witnessed the climax of the picture. This arises from their ignorance of literature and is, of course, their loss. Many good and extremely appropriate titles of this character are taken from the Psalms, from Shakespeare, and other poets. Frequently these quotations, used as titles, are so well known, and their meanings so apparent, that almost every one of the spectators will at once understand them, and catch at least the theme or general drift of the story from the title. Sometimes, again, the real significance of a title is best brought out by repeating it, or even the complete quotation from which it is taken, in the form of a leader at the point in the action where its significance cannot fail to be impressed upon the spectators. For example, a certain Selig release was entitled "Through Another Man's Eyes." Before the next to the last scene, which showed the ne'er-do-well lover peering in at the window, while his former friend bends over to kiss his wife—who might have been the wife of the wayward young man, had he been made of different stuff—the leader was introduced:

"How bitter a thing it is to look into happiness through another man's eyes!"

2. Elements of Plot

If it is important that, in every case, the spectators must be "shown" what happens in the working out of a plot, it is equally important that they be shown *why* it happens. This also has to do with sound and comprehensible motivation. "It is not so much a case of 'show me,' with the average American, as a common recognition that there must be a reason for the existence of everything created. He is inclined to give every play a fair show, will sit patiently through a lot of straining for effect, if there is a *raison d'être* in the summing up, but his mode of thought, and it belongs to the constitution of the race, is that of getting at some truth by venturesome experiment or logical demonstration."

7. Naming the Characters

One thing to be remembered, however, is that the picture spectators of today have been gradually educated up to expecting and approving many things which the spectators of a few years ago would have looked upon as too "highbrow." This is due in no small degree to the many screen adaptations of literary classics and fictional successes generally which have been made, as well as to the large number of stage plays that have been transferred to the screen, for, of course, the authors, publishers and dramatic producers have always stipulated that the casts be kept as they originally were made out—except that occasionally certain characters who in the stage-production of a certain play were merely spoken about and described have been, in the photoplay form, actually introduced, and thus added to the cast. But the point is that there is no longer the frantic striving to keep everything as "short and simple as possible" that once existed, and this applies to everything in the nature of inserts quite as much as to the names used for characters in the picture. Little by little "art" in motion picture production is becoming a reality instead of being merely a high-sounding word used occasionally by the press-agents.

13. Visions, Memories, Dreams, and Other Devices

Everyone who has attended the motion picture theatres has seen dozens of examples of "visions," produced in one or another manner, and it should be easy to distinguish between "visions" and "thoughts" or "memories." The latter *may* be introduced as part of another scene just as the vision (using the word in the sense of "apparition" or "supernatural visitant") is introduced; but it must be borne in mind that the photoplay spectators have in the past few years been gradually educated up to a rather perfect comprehension of what results different technical devices produce—even if they do not quite understand the technical why and wherefore; and for this reason it is best when writing action in which the characters are supposed to show what they are thinking about or describing to use the fade-out and fade-in device, as the meaning of this is now very clearly understood. The spectators are quite used to seeing the picture fade out, or "go black" at the end of certain scenes, just as they are familiar with the use of it at the actual end of the photoplay. Apart from these two uses, they have come to associate the fade-out with the thought[Pg 179] of the immediate introduction of a "memory," either related to others or silently indulged in, or a mere thought, or, if the character is seen going to sleep, of a "dream."

17. Serials

The future holds out immense possibilities for producers and writers of thoroughly good photoplay serials. Whereas in the past many serials were to be seen only in the second-rate houses, on account of the fact that their impossibly thrilling situations and weird plots appealed only to the juvenile and less intelligent spectators, now with the improvement in the *stories* of serial pictures has come an increase in the spectators who follow them up, and a consequent introduction of serials into theatres where at one time nothing of the kind would have been tolerated.

In conclusion, it may be said that for purposes of plot-study the photoplay serial can hardly be sur passed. Good, bad or indifferent, every photoplay serial reveals a sheer ingenuity of plotting that is a genuine inspiration to the writer of often better material. And a careful following-up and study of a *good* serial is a liberal photoplay-writing education in itself.

3. The Danger of Over-Compression

let us quote Mr. Frank E. Woods, who, besides being well known as a critic, photoplaywright, director and supervisor of productions under Mr. David W. Griffith, is an acknowledged expert in editing motion pictures.

"Many a picture," says Mr. Woods, "has been ruined by inadequate sub-titles. The makers of the picture have assumed that because *they* understood the meaning of every action, the spectators should also understand, forgetting that the spectators will view the picture for the first time. The moment a spectator becomes confused and loses the sense of what he is seeing on the screen, his interest is gone. While he is wondering 'What are they talking about now?' or 'Who is the chap in the long coat?' or 'How did he get from the house in the woods?' the film is being reeledoff merrily and the spectator has lost the thread of the story. Going to the other extreme and inserting sub-titles where the meaning is perfectly obvious, or telling in sub-titles that which is to be pictured immediately after, should also be avoided, although pictures are sometimes criticized for having too many titles when in fact the keen-eyed critic is the only one who finds them too many. The average spectator is none too alert.... The sub-title should be in complete harmony with the story and should never divert interest from the story. It should never be obtrusive. It should be there only because it belongs there. Therefore all sub-titles should be couched in language that harmonizes with the story. Every word should be weighed. Nothing should ever shock the spectator out of his interest in the picture by its incongruity, extravagance or inanity. Too much in a sub-title is as bad as too little—like seasoning in a pudding. The function of the sub-title is to supplement and correct the action of the picture, to cover lapses in the continuity, and to supply the finer shades of meaning which the actor has been unable to express in pantomime."

In passing, let us note one point of considerable moment. Notwithstanding the fact that many pictures are shown in which a leader immediately follows the title, it is much better not to arrange it so. Let your title be followed by a scene—by action—even though the scene be a short one. Then, if necessary, intro[Pg 228]duce your first leader. If when the photoplay opens the title is flashed upon the screen, and immediately a leader is shown, there is a chance that, having taken in the title almost at a glance, the spectator may momentarily divert his gaze and so miss your first leader, only turning his eyes toward the screen again when he notices that a scene is being shown. Again, even though he may be watching closely, the spectator is seldom quite so attentive to an explanatory insert which is shown before the opening scene as he is to one introduced later, when he has already become interested.

Most critics are also agreed that the use of leaders introducing the principal characters (usually accompanied by a few feet of film in which the character named is also pictured, perhaps in the act of bowing to the audience, or in some pose characteristic of the part he plays) is a mistake, when such "introducing" is done before the first scene of the story has been shown. Undoubtedly *anything* coming before the first scene is really out of place—so far as its being part of the story is concerned. Again Mr. Sargent stated a fact when he said that "What goes before the first real scene of a story is no more a part of that story than the design-head is a part of the fiction story. No magazine editor expects the author to be his own artist and supply an illustrated title. Start your story with the first scene of action, and let the director supply the preliminary scenes [close-ups of the principals] and leaders to suit himself."

As a matter of fact, though, the very best reason for not introducing from three to six or eight characters before the opening scene is that by the time the story has advanced a little many of the spectators have forgotten "who is who," whereas they have a much better opportunity to fix a character's name and occupation—so to speak—in their minds if that character is briefly but properly introduced at the point of his first entrance into the action of the play. Only the fact that we were already familiar with the faces of the contemporary historical characters shown in such features as Ambassador Gerard's "My Four Years in Germany" made it possible for us to keep track, during the first few scenes in which each one appeared, of the persons shown. No one could possibly have memorized the "panoramic" leader giving the cast, with its thirty or more names of characters and players.

8. Write Mainly of Characters That Arouse the Spectator's Sympathy

Each hero must have his opposite, as each great cause must have its protagonist and antagonist. Indeed, as we have seen, it is this warfare that makes all drama possible. But it will not do to glorify the doer of evil deeds and thus corrupt the sympathies of the spectators. The hero and not the "villain" must swing the sympathies of those who see. Be certain, therefore, that pity for, and even sympathy with, a wrong-doer is not magnified, through the action of your play, into admiration by the onlookers, for in the photoplay as in the legitimate drama the leading character may be a great offender. This way danger lies, however, and you must walk with extreme caution, or the censors "will catch you—if you don't watch out!"—to say nothing of the lashings of your own conscience.

Without repeating what was said in Chapter XVI regarding the introduction of crime into film stories, we would impress upon the photoplaywright the necessity for always having a fully sufficient, though not necessarily a morally justifiable, motive for any crime that is introduced in a story; besides, the introduction of a crime must be necessary to the action and not a mere spectacular scene. But remember that it is not sufficient to avoid "crime without motive;" the motive must be one which will, after the crime has been committed, leave no doubt in the mind of the spectator that the crime was virtually inevitable, if not absolutely unavoidable. If it is the hero of the story who commits the crime, the very greatest care must be taken to show that he had a really powerful motive for his act, if he is to have the sympathy—though not the approval—of the audience after yielding to temptation. This, of course, does not refer to deeds of violence which are really not only excusable but actually right, in the circumstances—like the killing of an attacking desperado in self-defense.

As an example of the point we are trying to emphasize, take a story like "The Bells," the play in which Sir Henry Irving appeared so often. Mathias the innkeeper, who later became the Burgomaster, was a character, who, by reason of Irving's superb art, won and held the sympathies of the audience from the start. Yet after Mathias had murdered the Polish Jew and robbed him of his belt of gold, even the art of Irving could not have made us sympathize with the character had we not been shown that Mathias was urged on to his crime—a crime for which he was constantly tortured ever afterward, and which occasioned his tragic death—by two very compelling motives. His primary motive was the urgent need of money. But he had a two-fold need of money: he had been notified by the landlord that he must pay his over-due rent or be turned out of his home; and he had been told by the doctor that unless he could immediately remove his sick wife to a milder climate she would certainly die. Thus, impelled by the thought that only by the speedy acquisition of sufficient money could he hope to save the life of his wife, he commits the deed which he would never have committed had his only motive been the necessity for raising money to pay the rent. Mathias was esteemed by his neighbors as an honest man; he was a man whose conscience smote him terribly when he was contemplating the murder of the Jew; and after the crime had been committed—fifteen years later, in fact—that same guilty conscience, wracking his very soul, drove him on to his death.

Shakespeare's Macbeth is a character with whom we are forced to sympathize measurably, because we know that he is not naturally a criminal. Yet, after all, Macbeth is a man who—as Professor Pierce has pointed out—"has been restrained in the straight path of an upright life [only] by his respect for conventions." Mathias, on the other hand, is not held in check by conventions; he is *essentially* an honest man. He commits a crime, but what stronger motive could a man have than the one that drove him on to its commission? And yet—and this is the mistake that we wish to point out to the young writer—seven years ago a certain company released "The Bells" as a two-part subject, in which, according to the synopsis published in the trade journals, Mathias's only motive for committing the most detestable of all crimes was that he was behind in his rent! Even the magazine that gave in fiction form the story of the picture failed to mention what is brought out so strongly in the play—the innkeeper's distress at the thought that his wife's life depended upon his being able to raise the money to send her to the south of France without delay. The author *mentioned* that Mathias had a sick wife, but that was all. The whole treatment of the story in fiction form, moreover, was farcical, such names as "Mr. Parker" being intermingled with those of the well-known characters, "Mathias," "Christian," and "Annette," while the wealthy, dignified Polish Jew was turned into a typical East-side clothing merchant. The real fault lay with the producer who, ignoring the great and pressing necessity that prompted Mathias's crime, garbled the original plot to the extent of allowing the innkeeper to murder the Jew because (according to the fiction-version in the magazine) he needed one hundred and seventy-five dollars to pay the rent! First, last, and all the time you must remember that your story *is not* a good story if the leading character is not, at all times, deserving of the spectator's sympathy, even when his action is not worthy of approval.

It is a matter for real regret to have to be compelled to state that, in spite of the many artistic advances made in motion-picture production during the past six or seven years, this most important point was deliberately overlooked when the Pathé Company made its very fine feature-production of "The Bells" in the Fall of 1918. We say "deliberately overlooked" because the writer who prepared the scenario for this modern five-reel version had the same opportunity as had the scenarioist who made the other adaptation, years ago, to read the original stage-play and to introduce this most compelling motive for Mathias's crime. If anything, the fault is more glaring in the Pathé production than in the older picture, for the wife is shown as a woman in apparently perfect health, although naturally worried by the fact that her husband's inability to raise the required amount of money may result in their losing both their home and their means of livelihood. All the fine acting of Mr. Frank Keenan as Mathias, and all the wonderful scenic and lighting effects, were not sufficient to make us lose sight of the fact that the ones responsible for the picture's production had not given proper thought to the necessity for showing that the innkeeper had an unusually compelling motive for taking the life of and then robbing his guest. And, make no mistake, no matter how fine the production may be in other respects, this sort of thing is not overlooked by the intelligent, right-minded spectator of the photoplay.

***

source : J. Berg Esenwein and Arthur Leeds, *Writing the photoplay*. Éditeur: Springfield, 1919.

6

Technique of the Photoplay

It does not matter how well you may write. The public does not want and will not have a succession of stories in which the heroine is drowned in the last fifty feet or where the hero commits suicide in the last ten. You will doubtless see many stories with unhappy and doleful endings on the screen. Some of them will be unusually good, but a majority will show on study that a half-baked author sought to be strong merely by being perverse and running contrary to the desire of his spectators.

Page -81-

To sell a story you must have either a new plot or a new use of an old idea. Since the new idea scarcely seems to exist, you must learn to make old ideas look so new that spectators are convinced that they are new.

Page -155-

The more compact your cast; the more closely your action is centered upon a few persons, the greater opportunity do you have for winning favor or disfavor for them. Employ this opportunity to the full. Center all the interest on the handful of major people you employ and do not confuse your story and the spectator by bringing in people who appear only on one action or sequence of scenes and are not heard of again. If you do this you will leave your spectators wondering what happened to this person or that.

Page -157-

And lastly, remember in writing action that if your action is important and it is necessary that it be clearly conveyed to the audience, it is necessary to play that action on the photographic stage where it may be seen to the best advantage. This must be done without seeming to make an effort to bring the players down front. If for any reason you must play an action well up stage and cannot bring the players down front, create a new stage wherever they may happen to be by writing a close-up of that part of the scene. If the action is a big one, depending upon the action of players in the mass, it does not have to be played upon the photographic stage; but where the expression of the individual player is largely instrumental in conveying the meaning of the action to the spectator this expression must be registered by the camera that the spectator may understand what it is about. If you can bring them down front do so. If you cannot, resort to a close-up. It is better to make a little trouble for the company than a great deal for the spectators the world over.

Page -275-

Next to the danger of selecting a theme dangerous in that it will antagonize the members of a sect or religious belief, the thing most to be feared is making the personages in j^our play of secondary importance to the problem it presents. This is a very common but none the less a grave error. A problem can possess only an academic interest. It must be made human by the personages whose adventures present the problem. In the presentation of your play you must first write your drama and then through our interest in these personages of the drama interest your spectators in the problem that their adventures present, but hold always to the problem.

Louis Lumière et son appareil : les spectateurs munis de lunettes spéciales [photographie de presse] / Agence Meurisse [BNF. MEU 105550 A-5080 bis B] 26 février 1935.

***

source : Epes Winthrop Sargent, *The technique of the photoplay*. New York City : The Moving picture world, 1913.

7

Practical Cinematography

Profit and pleasure combine to win recruits for the art of animated photography. As an entertainment offered to the public, the moving-pictures have had no rival. Their popularity has been remarkable and universal. It increases daily, and, since we are only now beginning to see the magnitude of what the cinematograph can effect, it is not likely to diminish. This development has stirred the ambition of the amateur or independent photographer because the field is so vast, fertile, and promising. Remunerative reward is obtainable practically in every phase of endeavour so long as the elements of novelty or originality are manifest. The result is that it is attracting one and all. Animated photography can convey so fascinating and convincing a record of scenes and events that many persons—sportsmen, explorers, and travellers—make use of it.

ATTRACTIONS AND OPPORTUNITIES OF THE ART

From the commercial point of view the issue is one of magnetic importance. In all quarters there is an increasing demand for films of prominent topical interest, either of general or local significance.

The proprietors of picture palaces have discovered that no films draw better audiences than these. If they deal with a prominent incident ike a visit of royalty to the neighbourhood, an important sporting event, a public ceremony, or even, such is human nature, with some disaster to life or property, they will make a stronger appeal for a few days than the general film fare offered at the theatre, because the episode which is uppermost in the mind of the public is what draws and compels public attention. Even, it would seem, when the reality itself has just been witnessed by the audience, its photographic reproduction proves more attractive than all else.

The picture palace, indeed, is assuming the functions of the illustrated newspaper, and is governed by like laws. The more personal and immediate the news, the more pleased are the beholders. So there is an increasing effort to supply upon the screen in life and motion what the papers are recording in print and illustration. One can almost hear the phrase that will soon become general, "Animated news of the moment." Already the French are showing us the way. In Paris one is able to visit a picture palace for 25 centimes at any time between noon and midnight and see, upon the screen, the events of the hour in photographic action. As fresh items of news, or, rather, fresh sections of film, are received, they are thrown upon the screen in the pictorial equivalent of the paragraphs in the stop press column of the newspapers, earlier items of less interest being condensed or expunged in the true journalistic manner to allow the latest photographic intelligence to be given in a length consistent with its importance.

It is obvious that this branch of the business must fall largely into the hands of the unattached or independent worker, who bears the same relation to the picture palace as the outside correspondent to the newspaper. A firm engaged in supplying topical films cannot hope to succeed without amateur assistance. No matter how carefully and widely it distributes its salaried photographers, numberless events of interest are constantly happening—shipwrecks, accidents, fires, sensational discoveries, movements of prominent persons, and the like, at places beyond the reach of the retained cinematographer. For film intelligence of these incidents the firm must rely upon the independent worker.

Curiously enough, in many cases, the amateur not only executes his work better than his salaried rival, but often outclasses him in the very important respect that he is more enterprising. Acting on his own responsibility, he knows that by smartness alone can he make wayagainst professionals. Only by being the first to seize a chance can he find a market for his wares. Thus when Blériot crossed the English Channel in his aeroplane it was the camera of an amateur that caught the record of his flight for the picture palaces, although a corps of professionals was on the spot for the purpose. True, the successful film showed many defects. But defects matter little compared with the importance of getting the picture first or exclusively. Similar cases exist in plenty. The amateur has an excellent chance against the professional. His remuneration, too, is on a generous scale. The market is so wide and the competition is so keen, especially in London, which is the world's centre of the cinematograph industry, that the possessor of a unique film can dictate his own terms and secure returns often twenty times as great as the prime cost of the film he has used.

The conveyance of players to a suitable natural setting is expensive, but it represents all the difference between success and failure. Of course, there are occasions when a natural setting demands a certain amount of artificial embellishment. This was the case in the filming of Hamlet, as presented by Sir Forbes Robertson and his company. A sea background and a battlemented castle were required. The former was quite easy to find, but the combination of the two was more difficult. The problem was solved by the choice of Lulworth Cove as the scene and by erecting a solid set to represent the castle. In this case the preparation of the extemporised castle was so thorough and careful that it looks like a weather-beaten stone building.

The photo-play stage will be forced to emulate the current practice of the theatre. It must bring the artist to bear upon the work. At the moment it is merely a combination of the photographer and the stage-manager or producer. The latter is not always an artist, though he is clever at making existing facilities suit his purpose. The theatre is holding its own principally because it respects the artistic side of the issue. Individuality is encouraged. The photo-play stage will have to follow the same line of action. Directly this is done the picture palace will become a spirited rival of the theatre.

For this reason the efforts of Sir Hubert von Herkomer, the eminent British artist, are being followed with interest. He was attracted to the photo-play producing business owing to the artistic atrocities perpetrated by the professional producer of film plays. He is not attempting to achieve any revolution, except in the mounting and acting of plays for the camera, but in this sphere he hopes to bring about a recognition of the part that the artist must play.

There is a complete absence of sensationalism about the artist-producer's work, and in this respect he goes against the conventions. He is deliberately flouting many of the accepted tenets of the photo-play production, and his attitude is certain to meet with some hostile criticism. But from the realist point of view he is correct. His matter-of-fact productions give verisimilitude to the scene and story, and brings them within the range of probability. There is no straining after effect. No detail is introduced unless it has a distinct bearing on the subject. The costumes are faithful to the last button. If a sixteenth century farmhouse is wanted, it is built, and built so well that in the picture it has every appearance of having been built of stone.

A feature which will be appreciated in the Herkomer productions is the suppression of the harsh and distressing blacks, greys and whites, which under brilliant illumination often convey the impression of snow. Nor do the players seem to be suffering from anęmia. These appear to be trivial matters in themselves, but they greatly affect the ultimate

whole. The robust aspect of the peasant who lives out of doors is faithfully conveyed, and he is thrown up in sharp contrast to the white-faced townsman. In the conventional picture-play, on the other hand, there is no individuality of facial expression, because one and all are made up in the same way.

Sir Hubert von Herkomer has commenced his work in a logical way. He confesses that until he began it he knew nothing about it. He was not harassed by a partial knowledge of how things are done. He is essentially a pioneer, content to work out his own ideas, and possessed of views upon stage-craft which are not to be despised. They had a good effect upon the theatre twenty or thirty years ago, and have lately been revived by another enthusiast. So Sir Hubert von Herkomer is not likely to be the slave of tradition.

He maintains that in the average photo-play everything is sacrificed to rapid action. This is true, and it is done purposely to distract attention from the weakness of the rest. The spectator must fix is attention upon the characters or he loses the thread of the story. No time is given him to see the deficiency of atmosphere or environment. The result is that everything is rushed through as if the villain and hero were racing the clock. To realise this it is only necessary to follow the film-play of a well-known historical story. Familiarity with the incident here gives the spectator a chance of taking in the setting and the mounting. If there are mistakes, interest gives way to mirth and all concentration is lost. The picture is followed with no more enthusiasm than a pantomime. This is the main reason why producers are chary of portraying well-known historical episodes upon the screen.

***

source : Frederick Arthur Ambrose Talbot, *Practical cinematography and its applications*. Philadelphia : J.B. Lippincott ; London : William Heinemann, 1913

8

The Photoplay (Master's thesis, 1914)

Avoid the commonplace; we are all familiar with the conventional. An erroneous idea entertained by many writers is that crime is the basis of all dramatic action. Too much stress can not be placed upon the desirability of avoiding crime, domestic infidelity, and related subjects as bases for scenarios. These subjects are distasteful to an audience, and should be shunned for the further reason that a severe censorship is placed upon the moving picture, and the portrayal of incidents repulsive to our sense of morals will eliminate an otherwise meritorious scenario. [...] Here the fact of the robbery is effectually conveyed to the audience without the action of the robbery being thrown upon the screen. It requires skillful handling of the plot to even suggest crime, and it is best omitted.

Page -17-

Your leading characters should appear early in the action of the play, and the audience immediately acquainted with their positions and connections with the plot. Their identity should be made apparent from the first; if the action of the play is incapable of such construction that this end is readily accomplished, resort to captions, as, for example, "Ethel's Brother Returns From College." Under no circumstances permit a character to leave the scene before his connection with the plot has been definitely impressed upon the audience.

Page -18-

The settings must be in harmony with the action of your play. Do not engage your characters in pursuits inconsistent with their station in life. A supposedly low-salaried character shown as a member of an exclusive club elicits criticism and weakens your plot. Nor would the matriculation of a day-laborer's daughter in a fashionable boarding school escape comment from what often proves to be a hypercritical audience. Remember that the evolution of the photoplay and the present demand for closer attention to details has sharpened the critical vision of even the casual witness of the "movies."

***

source : James A Taylor, "The Photoplay", Master's thesis (1914)

9

The Art of the Moving Picture

Written in 1915, The Art of the Moving Picture *by poet Vachel Lindsay is one of the first book to treat movies as art. Lindsay writes a brilliant analysis of the early silent films (including several now lost films). He is extraordinarily prescient about the future of moviemaking particularly about the business, the prominence of technology, and the emergence of the director as the author of the film.*

THE PHOTOPLAY OF ACTION

Let us assume, friendly reader, that it is eight o'clock in the evening when you make yourself comfortable in your den, to peruse this chapter. I want to tell you about the Action Film, the simplest, the type most often seen. In the mind of the habitué of the cheaper theatre it is the only sort in existence. It dominates the slums, is announced there by red and green posters of the melodrama sort, and retains its original elements, more deftly handled, in places more expensive. The story goes at the highest possible speed to be still credible. When it is a poor thing, which is the case too often, the St. Vitus dance destroys the pleasure-value. The rhythmic quality of the picture-motions is twitched to death. In the bad photoplay even the picture of an express train more than exaggerates itself. Yet when the photoplay chooses to behave it can reproduce a race far more joyously than the stage. On that fact is based the opportunity of this form. Many Action Pictures are indoors, but the abstract theory of the Action Film is based on the out-of-door chase. You remember the first one you saw where the policeman pursues the comical tramp over hill and dale and across the town lots. You remember that other where the cowboy follows the horse thief across the desert, spies him at last and chases him faster, faster, faster, and faster, and finally catches him. If the film was made in the days before the National Board of Censorship, it ends with the cowboy cheerfully hanging the villain; all details given to the last kick of the deceased.

One of the best Action Pictures is an old Griffith Biograph, recently reissued, the story entitled "Man's Genesis." In the time when cave-men-gorillas had no weapons, Weak-Hands (impersonated by Robert Harron) invents the stone club. He vanquishes his gorilla-like rival, Brute-Force (impersonated by Wilfred Lucas). Strange but credible manners and customs of the cave-men are detailed. They live in picturesque caves. Their half-monkey gestures are wonderful to see. But these things are beheld on the fly. It is the chronicle of a race between the brain of Weak-Hands and the body of the other, symbolized by the chasing of poor Weak-Hands in and out among the rocks until the climax. Brain desperately triumphs. Weak-Hands slays Brute-Force with the startling invention. He wins back his stolen bride, Lily-White (impersonated by Mae Marsh). It is a Griffith masterpiece, and every actor does sound work. The audience, mechanical Americans, fond of crawling on their stomachs to tinker their automobiles, are eager over the evolution of the first weapon from a stick to a hammer. They are as full of curiosity as they could well be over the history of Langley or the Wright brothers.

The dire perils of the motion pictures provoke the ingenuity of the audience, not their passionate sympathy. When, in the minds of the deluded producers, the beholders should be weeping or sighing with desire, they are prophesying the next step to one another in worldly George Ade slang. This is illustrated in another good Action Photoplay: the dramatization of The Spoilers. The original novel was written by Rex Beach. The gallant William Farnum as Glenister dominates the play. He has excellent support. Their team-work makes them worthy of chronicle: Thomas Santschi as McNamara, Kathlyn Williams as Cherry Malotte, Bessie Eyton as Helen Chester, Frank Clark as Dextry, Wheeler Oakman as Bronco Kid, and Jack McDonald as Slapjack.

There are, in The Spoilers, inspiriting ocean scenes and mountain views. There are interesting sketches of mining-camp manners and customs. There is a well-acted love-interest in it, and the element of the comradeship of loyal pals. But the chase rushes past these things to the climax, as in a policeman picture it whirls past blossoming gardens and front lawns till the tramp is arrested. The difficulties are commented on by the people in the audience as rah-rah boys on the side lines comment on hurdles cleared or knocked over by the men running in college field-day. The sudden cut-backs into side branches of the story are but hurdles also, not plot complications in the stage sense. This is as it should be. The pursuit progresses without St. Vitus dance or hysteria to the end of the film. There the spoilers are discomfited, the gold mine is recaptured, the incidental girls are won, in a flash, by the rightful owners.

These shows work like the express elevators in the Metropolitan Tower. The ideal is the maximum of speed in descending or ascending, not to be jolted into insensibility. There are two girl parts as beautifully thought out as the parts of ladies in love can be expected to be in Action Films. But in the end the love is not much more romantic in the eye of the spectator than it would be to behold a man on a motorcycle with the girl of his choice riding on the same machine behind him. And the highest type of Action Picture romance is not attained by having Juliet triumph over the motorcycle handicap. It is not achieved by weaving in a Sherlock Holmes plot. Action Picture romance comes when each hurdle is a tableau, when there is indeed an art-gallery-beauty in each one of these swift glimpses: when it is a race, but with a proper and golden-linked grace from action to action, and the goal is the most beautiful glimpse in the whole reel.

In the Action Picture there is no adequate means for the development of any full grown personal passion. The distinguished character-study that makes genuine the personal emotions in the legitimate drama, has no chance. People are but types, swiftly moved chessmen. More elaborate discourse on this subject may be found in chapter twelve on the differences between the films and the stage. But here, briefly: the Action Pictures are falsely advertised as having heart-interest, or abounding in tragedy. But though the actors glower and wrestle and even if they are the most skilful lambasters in the profession, the audience gossips and chews gum.

Why does the audience keep coming to this type of photoplay if neither lust, love, hate, nor hunger is adequately conveyed? Simply because such spectacles gratify the incipient or rampant speed-mania in every American.

To make the elevator go faster than the one in the Metropolitan Tower is to destroy even this emotion. To elaborate unduly any of the agonies or seductions in the hope of arousing lust, love, hate, or hunger, is to produce on the screen a series of misplaced figures of the order Frankenstein.

How often we have been horrified by these galvanized and ogling corpses. These are the things that cause the outcry for more censors. It is not that our moral codes are insulted, but what is far worse, our nervous systems are temporarily racked to pieces. These wriggling half-dead men, these over-bloody burglars, are public nuisances, no worse and no better than dead cats being hurled about by street urchins.

The cry for more censors is but the cry for the man with the broom. Sometimes it is a matter as simple as when a child is scratching with a pin on a slate. While one would not have the child locked up by the chief of police, after five minutes of it almost every one wants to smack him till his little jaws ache. It is the very cold-bloodedness of the proceeding that ruins our kindness of heart. And the best Action Film is impersonal and unsympathetic even if it has no scratching pins. Because it is cold-blooded it must take extra pains to be tactful. Cold-blooded means that the hero as we see him on the screen is a variety of amiable or violent ghost. Nothing makes his lack of human charm plainer than when we as audience enter the theatre at the middle of what purports to be the most passionate of scenes when the goal of the chase is unknown to us and the alleged "situation" appeals on its magnetic merits. Here is neither the psychic telepathy of Forbes Robertson's Cæsar, nor the fire-breath of E.H. Sothern's Don Quixote. The audience is not worked up into the deadly still mob-unity of the speaking theatre.

We late comers wait for the whole reel to start over and the goal to be indicated in the preliminary, before we can get the least bit wrought up. The prize may be a lady's heart, the restoration of a lost reputation, or the ownership of the patent for a churn. In the more effective Action Plays it is often what would be secondary on the stage, the recovery of a certain glove, spade, bull-calf, or rock-quarry. And to begin, we are shown a clean-cut picture of said glove, spade, bull-calf, or rock-quarry. Then when these disappear from ownership or sight, the suspense continues till they are again visible on the screen in the hands of the rightful owner.

In brief, the actors hurry through what would be tremendous passions on the stage to recover something that can be really photographed. For instance, there came to our town long ago a film of a fight between Federals and Confederates, with the loss of many lives, all for the recapture of a steam-engine that took on more personality in the end than private or general on either side, alive or dead. It was based on the history of the very engine photographed, or else that engine was given in replica. The old locomotive was full of character and humor amidst the tragedy, leaking steam at every orifice. The original is in one of the Southern Civil War museums. This engine in its capacity as a principal actor is going to be referred to more than several times in this work.

The highest type of Action Picture gives us neither the quality of Macbeth or Henry Fifth, the Comedy of Errors, or the Taming of the Shrew. It gives us rather that fine and special quality that was in the ink-bottle of Robert Louis Stevenson, that brought about the limitations and the nobility of the stories of Kidnapped, Treasure Island, and the New Arabian Nights.

This discussion will be resumed on another plane in the eighth chapter: Sculpture-in-Motion.

Having read thus far, why not close the book and go round the corner to a photoplay theatre? Give the preference to the cheapest one. *The Action Picture will be inevitable. Since this chapter was written, Charlie Chaplin and Douglas Fairbanks have given complete department store examples of the method, especially Chaplin in the brilliantly constructed Shoulder Arms, and Fairbanks in his one great piece of acting, in The Three Musketeers.*

***

Source : Vachel Lindsay, *The art of the moving picture*. New York: Macmillan, 1915

10

Psychology of the Screen

If you get out Volume P.o of that new *Encyclopedia Brittanica*, that you're buying at a dollar down and a dollar ever afterwards, you'll find that the subject of this article isn't so hard as it looks. Reduced to brass tacks, it simply means the way the brain works — my brain, your brain, and the brain of your next-door neighbor (provided he has one). And so the psychology of the screen means the way the Motion Picture actors and actresses express the emotions that are supposed to be going on in their minds — love, maybe ; and how some of those beyoutiful heroes and heroines do express that — wheel — or hate, or jealousy, or despair because the cook is leaving — and the way they make these emotions reach out across the orchestra and set the fat drummer in the third row blubbering, or the highschool girl and her beau to holding hands.

In the spoken drama, the audience is continually being coached and directed how to feel. The characters of the play explain and argue and scatter words right and left in the most spendthrift fashion. When the playwright is afraid his audience wont understand the heroine's state of mind, he simply sets the butler and the maid to tidying up the drawing-room to the accompaniment of a conversation something like this :

The Butler (shaking head mournfully) — It fair breaks me heart to see how unhappy the mistress is these days!

The Maid (dusting a papier-mache bust of Lincoln)

— Yes, it's because she's too stout to wear this season's styles. She's afraid she'll have to give up icecream sundaes to keep master's love. What brutes you men are!

—an so on, until every one knows the whole situation. Now, on the screen it is difficult for an actess to behave like a woman who has had to give up ice-cream sundaes, or yet as somebody or other has suggested to enter the room with the air of just having had a cup of tea.

Subtleties like these are too fine for the screen. If the movie audiences are to understand what is going on, only the most elementary and recognizable emotions can be chosen for photoplay use. We've all of us presumably experienced love, remorse, jealousy and sorrow at some time in our lives, and it's dollars to doughnuts we'll know them when we see them. When the handsome hero with the square jaw kisses the lovely heroine with the expensive hair, Friend Wife leans against our shoulder and murmurs, tenderly, "He doesn't do it half so well as you did, Jim; and I dont see — do you ? — why they call her so goodlooking!" And when the villain repents, and dies to slow music, we remember the time we gave a lead nickel to the conductor, and feel for our handkerchiefs in real sympathy.

A few years ago, photoplays were mostly pictures of action, cowboys and Indians on horseback, guns going off, trains being wrecked, autos speeding after fugitives, and "something doing" generally. But people got sick and tired of Chief Rain-in-the-Face and his band of Irish-American Indians, and gun-fights — with the pianist bearing hard on the bass — ceased to thrill. So the word went forth to the scenario writers to work a little plot and heart-interest into their scripts. The "picture-play" became the "silent drama," and the movie actors found that it was distinctly up to them to register a large number of emotions, so that they would "get over" to their audiences.

Lacking words, the picture people adopted a sort of shorthand code of gesture to represent different emotions, and the faithful fans have learnt this code by heart. When the persecuted heroine clutches her chest and rolls her eyes, they know she is not having an attack of acute indigestion, but a pang of unrequited affection. When the hero beats his brow and clenches his fist, they know it is not the bill for his wife's new hat that troubles him, but the fact that he has just dropped a couple of millions in Wall Street. Jealousy has its bitten lip ; revenge, its flashing eye and set jaw.

When Theda Bara lets down her back hair and runs her hands thru it, in a sort of vampirish shampoo, it is a sign that she is being very naughty.

I dont quite know why back hair is as naughty as it is, but when a movie actress lets hers down, it's one of the surest things you know that trouble is brewing. Likewise when she smooths it straight back, a la Yaleska Suratt, or parts it and rolls it very low, so that it hides her ears.

When Edith Storey's sensitive nostrils quiver and her eyes dilate, the fan recognizes her portrayal as that of dread. And when Charlie Chaplin stumbles onto the screen, with his million-dollar mustache, he gets a laugh before he earns it, because, in the code of moviedom, a stumble and tumble and ten-cent-store scrap of whisker is mighty humorous.

To be sure, some people do not recognize this code at once. When you take dear old Aunt Matilda from back home to the Motion Pictures, and she sees Charlie Chaplin playfully kick a lady in the stomach, it is just possible that she may nudge you and inquire, anxiously :

"What are all the folks laughing at, anyhow, Lizzie? Why, ef that young feller should cut-up round Green Corners scand'lous as that, the seelect men would put him in the jail."

Come to think of it, I'm blest if I know why a short man in baggy trousers, kicking out with a shoe two sizes too large, is so uproariously funny ; but it must be, for Charlie gets seven times as much money as the President of the United States every year for doing it. You point out this fact to Aunt Matilda, and when a little later Charlie upsets a perambulator with the crook of his cane, the good . old soul is quite convulsed with merriment.

Memory is perhaps the most important function the brain of man performs. Our emotions are nearly all of them dependent on the process of remembering — of tying the present to the past. We cannot hate very cordially without memory ; we cannot love successfully, nor hope, nor grieve. A baby's worn shoe is not a pathetic or tender object unless it makes us remember some child we have loved or lost ; a rose is significant to a lover because of its connection with past love-episodes ; the knife is terrible to a criminal because of the association it has with his crime.

In the representation of this most universal process of psychology, the photoplay has the advantage of the spoken drama. It can picture to the spectator the actual scene that is being recalled to the hero or heroine's mind. In Vitagraph's "The Man Who Couldn't Beat God," the man's conscience-tortured brain is bared to the gaze of the audience. He has thought about his old crime so much that sick memory twists ordinary, everyday happenings inte visions of his victim. . Finally, sitting in a box at a performance of "Oliver Twist," he sees Bill Sykes murdering his light-o'-love, Nancy, and rises up with an irresistible cry of warning and confession. No mere pantomime could portray this man's emotions without the aid of camera trickery. But the "doubleexposure," with its possibilities of representing dreams, hallucinations and memories, has done much to change mere Motion Pictures into emotion pictures with dramatic possibilities of spiritual and mental conflict.

Partly on account of this trick work, the camera is more successful in portraying abnormal phases of the mind than normal ones, the heightened emotions than the simpler and commoner feelings. Thus love makes a better picture-theme than affection or friendship, sorrow than grief, and jealousy than doubt. Of course leaders are often used to explain emotions that cannot very well be visualized, but leaders at their best are boesome affairs, and at their worst they are impertinent interruptions. Two longseparated lovers at last reach each other's arms, but before their lips can meet, the inconsiderate director cuts them off with a remark something on this order :

> The Misunderstanding Between Grace and Tom Is Finally Removed.

A bank clerk, worried by the odd millions he had abstracted from the petty-cash drawer, is about to end his troubles with a pistol, and again that busybody of a director interrupts at the crucial point with a leader anent the wage's of sin. No, no ; as few leaders as possible, if you please, Mr. Photoplaywright, and, if they are necessary, make them at least truer to life than they are now.

A little care taken to make not only the leaders but the letters or newspaper notices shown in the plays more convincing would help a great deal toward improving the psychology of the screen. As it is now, the characters commit the most dangerous secrets to paper, and conveniently lose the paper for some other character to find. Crooks communicate freely by letter, prattling artlessly of murder and robbery ; young ladies leave their love-notes about, to be found by irate parents or husbands, and a man informs his wife of his plans as follows (in backhand grammar-school script) :

Dear Wife: Am leaving on business for China at two o'clock. Will be back a year from next January.

Your affectionate husband,

Bob.

The psychology of the screen is at present a rather elementary psychology, but one in a wonderful process of development. Its success depends upon the collaboration of the spectator with the playwright in supplying, imagining and interpreting what he cannot say. For this reason it is a valuable aid to concentration and alertness of understanding. In a way, when you and I go to a photoplay, we are author and actor and audience, too, like that famous individual of the Bab Ballads, who was "cap'n and cook and bo'sun, too and crew of the Nancy's brig!

***

source : Anonymous, "Psychology of the Screen". *Motion Picture Classic* (1916)

MOTION PICTURE
CLASSIC
DECEMBER
25¢
Marian Nixon
Don Reed
Are American Movies Corrupting Japan?
GRAFTING FROM THE STARS

11

Movie Advertising viewed by a Fan

MOVIE ADVERTISING FROM THE VIEW POINT OF A FAN

You may hardly credit it when I say that motion-picture audiences are the most critical in the world. They do not outwardly show their disapproval of things, but after they resolved that the photoplay was here to stay, anything as a motion picture would no longer satisfy them. So the film producers had to humor the folks who had made their wealth, and today, the fans have been educated up to such a pitch that nothing but the best will satisfy them. Here, then, is the class of readers represented by moving-picture publicity.

The obvious conclusion is that advertisers will have to follow the path of the ordinary producer in order to obtain the greatest value out of this new advertising medium.

A talk with an intelligent motion-picture fan, as I found, is very interesting.

"I would like your views on ad. films," I asked.

"With pleasure/ she replied, and forthwith got down to business.

"I must say that they are considerably more interesting than the advertisements that meet your eye in the newspapers. How nice it is to watch an industry on the screen and be taken through a big manufacturing plant. It is an education in itself, and it never strikes you as though it was intended as a boost, although the particular thing the point the advertiser wishes to bring home, I believe you call it leaves an indelible impression on you".

"I also enjoy the films in which there is a story. One such film, I remember, told of a poor family who took in washing. Disease abounded, and the folks who had their laundry done learned their lesson. Then the sanitary methods of the steam laundry were contrasted. It impressed me very much.

"The comic films are frequently laughable, but I remember being offended once at seeing a man like somebody s beer so much that he drank it until he was dead drunk. I noticed that I was not the only spectator to leave the hall. I like, at all times, my photoplay fare to be in good taste.

"At some of the movie theaters I at tend they make a practice of running a number of slides after the reels. They relate to neighboring stores, but are so dry and shown for so many weeks with out being changed that I always skip them."

"Would you prefer," I chimed in, "that the advertising film portion be abolished?"

"I would not so long as the ordinary pictures did not suffer in quality and quantity. A show I regularly visit out in New Jersey always runs the ad. films after the program has finished. As the pictures are invariably good ones, I always stay to see them through, and most others in the audience seem to do like wise. And another thing, the subjects are frequently changed, for naturally one grows tired of seeing the same things over and over again."

"Have you," I broached, "any suggestions for improvements?"

"Sure; I would like to see some of my favorite photoplayers take the leading parts in the ad. stories. It would be just crazy to watch Mary Fuller and Francis X. Bushman as a pair of newly weds who try to overcome housekeeping difficulties with various modern articles to be bought at stores.

"I also think that there is considerable room for improving the film plots. They should be as good as the ordinary photoplays. What they seem to lack is strength. There is seldom any of the strong, exciting situations which I am accustomed to see, and the punch is often conspicuous by its absence at the end."

APPROACHING THE WORKING CLASSES WITH A MOTION-PICTURE PLAY

It was the Bard of Stratford who said that "the play was the thing". Although it then referred to the legitimate stage, as it does now, it can to-day apply aptly to the motion-picture theater. A good story is, also, the ideal vehicle for film advertising.The twenty million movie fans in this country frequent their favorite form of amusement to be entertained, and some greatly resent the pure advertising or semi-educationals which they often have to sit out. It must be borne in mind that it is the one kind of relaxation by which the working classes are able to get away from the monotony and hardness of their everyday existence. They, therefore, want their fare served up in an appetizing manner. Anything else is apt to prove a bore, and you can thus see what kind of a receptive mood by which you have to approach the average motionpicture audience. That is why it is advisable to have your advertising points ingeniously incorporated in either a comedy or drama, the former preferably.The most common type of ad. film is the industrialog, portray-ing the processes by which certain goods are manufactured. Sev-eral of these subjects I have seen at the picture shows lately were so unnecessarily padded that they were enough to send spectators to sleep. No wise advertiser would attempt to cram in all the matter he could into the smallest possible space in his press announce-ments, neither should he try it on the film.

Industrialogs undoubtedly appeal more to a better-class audience, but it must be remembered that a good pro portion of the movie theaters are still nickel shows, which attract the working classes. These folks see enough of factory and business life in the daytime, so they do not want to be inflicted with it when endeavoring to get away from the atmosphere. Here you have a large audience which is extremely difficult to address via the press, for the majority go in for hardly any reading at all. May be they haven t got the inclination or money to do it. Their custom is certainly worth while cultivating, and no doubt they can understand pictures better than books, as, when the world was young, pictures were drawn on slabs of stone to indicate what otherwise could not be explained. Compelled to go out to work at an early age is responsible for a good proportion of the masses being poor readers and writers. By the motion pictures, however, you can approach public previously beyond your reach.

I recently was commissioned to write a short comedy scenario for a well-known tobacco manufacturer, and here follows the synopsis of the plot:

Bill, a workingman, is enjoying his pipe of Tobacco in the parlor of his home, when a passerby notices smoke issuing from the window. Thinking the house on fire, he brings the fire department on the scene. They turn the hose on the house, and, after a severe drenching, Bill escapes. He is indignant at being duped by the passerby, and the firemen also resent being made fools of. They then turn the hose on the culprit, who pleads for mercy. Bill offers to release him if he buys four packages of Tobacco all round. The passerby agrees, and hurries off to the shop to buy the same, pacifying his victims, who are left enjoying the tobacco.

For some things drama is better for hammering points home, but stick to comedy as much as you can it is more popular with movie audiences.

The French branch of the Remington Typewriter Company recently had a photoplay story produced which concerned a working girl, who, on her father s death, was the only support of the family. Through the firm cutting down expenses, she is dismissed and vainly endeavors to obtain another position as a stenographer. At the end of her resources, she obtains a Remington typewriter on the installment plan and obtains sufficient clients to provide her with work.

It is seldom advisable to go beyond a reel, which occupies about eighteen minutes on the screen, for that is the ideal length. Audiences will stand this with out a murmur of protest, since they appreciate one good extra reel on the pro gram. It matters little whether they realize that it is advertising disguised. Quick action is one of the things that have been responsible for the great present vogue of the motion picture, so have your producer compress all he can into every foot of film. It should then bring you more than the desired results.

***

Source : Ernest A. Dench : *Advertising by Motion Pictures.* Standard Publishing Co. : Cincinnati, Ohio, 1916

see also :

- Dench, Ernest A. : *Making the Movies.* Macmillan Co., New York, 1915 Dench, Ernest A.: *Motion Picture Education* . Standard Publishing Co.: Cincinnati, Ohio, 1917
- Dench, Ernest A.: *Putting your Library in the Movies.* In: The Library Journal. Vol. 43 – February 1918 (January-December, 1918). Publication Office: New York, 1919. – P. 71-73.

This is your Chance!
WILLIAM FOX
Presents
THEDA BARA
AS
CLEOPATRA
NOW PACKING THEATRES
AS A SPECIAL ATTRACTION
RELEASED IN AUGUST
ON A RENTAL BASIS.
Fix Your Bookings Today!
FOX
FILM CORPORATION
New Fox policy for 1918-19
announced next week -

12

Psychology of the movies

After spending five years with the intricacies of orange ranching, which intricacies included the big freeze, three floods, and a famine from scale, I returned to civilization, which is Los Angeles, to find the moving picture to be second only to the automobile in wonderful advancement during that five years. I immediately became a movie fan. My reasons for so doing were various. I had lost all sense of anticipation while ranching, because it is beyond human endeavor to anticipate what California will dish up in the shape of weather to an inoffensive orange grower. I had lost all hope because after having one flood wash me off the earth, I had had two more wash me practically out of existence, so I was hopeless, and I did not have an illusion left to my name.TTherefore I turned to the picture plays which are all illusion, to regain a normal state of mind. They proved to be worth while. — the moving pictures. They restored in a measure much I had lost in battling with the stern realities of ranching, and I became a regular patron to them for some time before I began to notice the audiences. Recently they have proved more interesting than the pictures.

What psychological effect will the movies have upon the present generation was naturally a question which arose in my mind as soon as I had grown rested and observant. I had come to them without much of anything left in my mind, except harassment. Being deprived of hope and anticipation and illusion one finds oneself bereft of about all that makes life worth while. I knew from hard experience that things do not come out right, regardless of how much one tries, so that at first the fact that every picture showed success for the ending, rather grated upon me, yet in course of time, I had that much of my illusions of life restored to me through the photo drama. I did not bring to the theater the absolute sophistication that seemed to mark the youngsters about me. They all knew exactly how every illusion in the picture is done. They know all the scenes shown. "That's the post-office at Topanga," "There is the road in Laurel Canyon," "I saw them taking that scene on Spring street," and "Say, he's no good, I know the feller that sells him his cigars," were comments freely made by members of the audience. Evidently, familiarity with the moving picture people and the California scenery has bred a certain amount of contempt in the youthful movie fan. Nothing of pleasure would seem to be left to them, because they know exactly what a villain does a certain thing for, and exactly what he will do next, and just how the heroine is going to escape. Why then do they attend? They can get no anticipation and no illusion from what they regard so cynically. If the youth of seventeen of today can be neither amused nor interested in what they see, what shall we expect of them at forty? Will they be the better off for having no illusions, no anticipations and no hopes when they are young, to be crushed by the stern realities, the hard failures, and the doubtful successes of life? This is a psychological development which it will be interesting to watch.

This youthful cynicism seems to be more prevalent in the higher-priced houses on Broadway than in the five-cent houses on the same thoroughfare. I have wondered about that. We go to see a star, and whatever he or she does, we accept as being the proper thing in photo-drama. Some of the things the stars are doing are really too absurd for words, so absurd that they are both clever and amusing, but not the slightest true to nature, nor to life. Then in some of the five cent houses they show just as absurd stuff, which is not greeted with laughter, but with guffaws at its absurdities, yet it is no more absurd than the stuff the stars are doing. But the class of people attending the five-cent shows is different from that which attends the ten, twenty, and thirty houses. It is not such a blase, sophisticated crowd.

It takes its shows more literally. It does not care how the picture is made. It is not looking at a picture. It is looking at life, and it wants its life pictures, true to life. It guffaws if it sees an absurdity upon life. It does not care who is doing the acting because what it is looking at is not acting but reality and it has kept its illusions, and anticipations, and its hopes and brings them to the show keyed up to the highest pitch. The audience in a five-cent show is the most interesting in the city. As a rule the houses are small, though showing fine pictures, and the voices of excited gazers can be heard throughout the place, and the comments made by them are funnier than a show, and the rabid desire of the young girls and women for murder, and revenge, and bloodletting is simply astounding! The young thing in front of me looks as though she would not hurt a fly, as though she would squeal at a mouse, and yet she sits watching two men knifing each other to death, drawing in her breath between her teeth, and shaking all over with excitement, and when the villain has been done to death by the trusty knife of the hero (I shudder to think what would happen to such an audience if by mistake the director had the hero done to death by the villain accidentally) she lets go of her breath, and says audibly to her escort, "My God, I'm glad he got him!"

And beside me sit two young things, a girl of seventeen and her sister of ten, and they watch the picture with much comment.

"Of course he loves her, and will get her. You watch him. Ain't he fine," the big sister admonishes. But obstacles to be overcome before he gets her are tremendous, and include a wonderful hair-breatdh escape from a pit of death, with the heroine tackled firmly to the hero's waist by rope while he digs his way up the crumbling sands. Every step of this perilous ascent is commented upon vividly by the two beside me, and when the hero slips with exhaustion and almost falls back into the abyss but is deftly caught by the heroine, (the sophisticated youth at the higher priced places would calmly tell vou how this was done, and would thereby miss the thrill of his life,) the older girl screams out, "I pray to God he saves her." Her prayer is answered, for of what use would a director be, if not to save the situation, but the girls beside me are not thinking of directors, nor of the story which must come out right. They are witnessing life, as real and absolute as though they were living it. Yet one wonders what such girls would actually do, if such calamities should touch them in real life. Perhaps they will wring life dry of all its emotions by photodrama, instead of reality. If so, they will have been spared much misery and afforded great pleasure.

The newcomers behind me are a fond hubby, an excitable wife, and a child. 'Now don't get excited," cautions hubby as wifey's breath goes with a sob. "Oh, why don't they go one," she pleads, as the picture flashes off at its most terrifying point, to show the caption, which she reads in a rush, and then must wait an interminable time until the rest of the audience has had time to read through. "I can't live if they don't go on," she wails. "Now don't get excited, darling," cautions the hubby again. 'Tt will all come back in a minute." "But I can't wait," shrills the woman, and the child asks anxiously, "Will he kill him, father; do you think he will kill him?" "Yes, yes, petty, y-e-s-s," replied the busy father. Comes back the picture, and a long drawn breath from the wife results. Then she begins to really get excited. Her voice rises. "Oh, why don't he strike? Oh, the big boob, can't he see the other feller is going to kill him? Oh, why don't he strike?" And of course he does strike, at the exact moment when he should, knowing all the time that the villain was behind him, and the woman cries out in delight, "Goody, goody, goody."

Now what do you think of that? What will the psychological effect be upon us as a race of people during the next ten or fifteen years ? We have got to be thrilled. In the higher priced houses, it must be absurdity that thrills us, stars shooting over office buildings, and jumping moving trains, taking flying leaps from automobiles over cliff's, anything so that it is of tremendous risks, and even then the sophisticated onlooker remarks that the trick was done so and so, yet he must have it even if tricks do it. In the cheaper houses, the thrills produced must be murder, and fights, and wife beating, and abuse of crippled children. It is the shilling shocker, the dime novel over again only a million times more intense. The youngsters so small they can not read the captions, go to see the pictures, and beg their elders to read 'what it says," and they are as excited and as thrilled as the older ones.

Think of the perverted emotions developed by the moving pictures, and then wonder what the effect at large will be. Yet the movie fan does not want a fine story, and fine acting, with fine ideals exploited. No, it wants its thrills and such thrills as they are likely never to experience in real life. For what one of us, looking at the pictures, expects to be held up and robbed, beaten by thugs, knifed by a jealous rival, or thrown over a cliff from an automobile as we go on our peaceful way homeward? The very premonition of any such disaster overtaking us would frighten us into seventeen different sorts of fits.

'Tis an odd phase of life we are living through. Has it anything to do with the amazing record of young criminals?

'Tis a problem perplexing very
To the cannibal maid, and the missionarv.'
Indeed it is.

***

Source: *The New American Woman*, Vol. III, 1, Feb. 1918, p. 19.

13

Developing Your Plot

Plot germs have taken up quite a bit of our time in this new series of thoughts on the writing of photoplays. And rightly so. For, unless you know where to look for plots, and how to recognize a possible plot in embryo, how are you going to construct them?

Let's proceed a step further along our path. Having discovered the germ of a plot, how are we going to develop it into a full-grown, vigorous structure? What is the prime necessity? What magic touch infuses life and strength into the bare idea we possess and makes of it something that will hold the interest of others, that will entertain them?

Speaking generally, and leaving to later discussion the narrower by-ways and paths of plot development, we may set down as the primary essential of a plot the basic element—*struggle.* Your plot germ, your original idea, is usually an out of the ordinary character or an incident that concerns ordinary characters in an unusual manner.

Into this source, you must inject—*struggle.* Some will call it *conflict*, others will tell you that *suspense* is the necessity. But suspense is the outgrowth of struggle or conflict.

There is struggle of varying sorts. Your struggle may be that between the different characters of your story, it may be the struggle of one of your characters against conditions of life and the world, it may be the struggle of your character with his own inner self.

But it is struggle of one sort or another that makes your story. Barring the few exceptions whose existence we have noted, and which we will describe and study later, it is the tale of struggles that makes up the entertainment of the world.

The spectator who comes to see a motion picture, or the reader who picks up a book, expects to be introduced to an interesting character, one whom he will either like very much or dislike very much. After hearing your premises they expect to witness a struggle, the further progress in life of your character and necessarily the sort of progress that brings struggle. Your character may be the most interesting one in the world, but two hours talk about his unusual points will not satisfy anyone. Those two hours must concern things that are happening to your character or events that he is causing to happen—that is, the element of struggle.

You will remember that last month, in discussing the possible plots to be discovered in newspapers, we found a germ in the "Letters From Readers" column. It was an epistle signed "Lonesome," and was from a young man who wanted to know why the big city did not provide some sort of welfare club or association where a stranger could meet and become acquainted with other persons?

That word "Lonesome" aroused our curiosity. It would likewise interest an audience. Imagine Charles Ray in the character. We see him fresh from the country, in his little hall-room, life, hustle and bustle all around him. But to Charlie they mean nothing; he has none in the length and breadth of the city to call "Friend."

When you have introduced such a character you have the audience with you. But you must go further. The audience wants to see Charlie struggle against his environment, or, out of his despair they wish to see him perform some rash act that will force a struggle on him.

Comedy or drama can be developed from such a theme—by the injection of struggle. The chances are you will bring to light the most artistic and desirable of blends —comedy-drama. Suppose that our "Lonesome" youngster, suddenly grown rash, forms a decision. "I'm going to walk out that door," he says, "and speak to the first person I meet. I don't care whether it's John D. Rockefeller or a street sweeper, I'm going to tell him I'm lonesome and want someone to talk to who will speak about something beside the weather." There's the start of your struggle. Why, it's a funny struggle alone to see Charlie walking the room, trying to screw up his determination to go through with the rashly made resolution. Finally he strides forth bravely.

Whom does he meet?

There's where your genius as a story teller comes in. What sort of a character would O. Henry have him meet? Start a Harold McGrath story off with this theme. The story will be running away with you—if your imagination is in working order.

The simplest form of struggle is that of the eternal triangle—two men for a girl, or the conflict of two women for one man. The struggle that develops out of your "Lonesome" story may eventuate in that sort before it gets very far. But you can see that you have started on more original ground, that if you follow these paths you will not have simply an "eternal triangle" story.

That has been our reason for withholding mention of "struggle" to this point. There are those who would tell you of this basic essential before any other point had been discussed. The result is that so many amateurs set out to write stories by seeking for a struggle. They look over the list of various sorts of struggles, two men for a girl, two girls for a man, man against poverty, man against temptations, and so on. And when the alleged story is completed it is merely a framework, without life or soul. Stilted characters struggle through time-worn situations.

"Struggle" may be classified and indexed. But "plot germs" cannot; the plot germs that *you* can discover are limited only by your own experience, your own reading, your own imagination. And if you set out to write your story by searching for the germ that is unusual and interesting, the chances are in your favor in securing originality—something different. Because *your own life*, your own viewpoint is something different. It is yours as long as you keep it yours, it is going to become trite only when you grow lazy and follow the lines of pictures and stories you remember because that is the easy way.

Starting with a germ that is *different, the "struggle" you provide will be different because it will* be the sort of struggle that could happen only to your *different* characters.

There's the basis of originality—your own life, your own heart, your own mind.

***

source : Anonymous. Developing Your Plot. *Film Truth*, Vol. 1, No. 6, September 1920.

The 1920s: The 4 Best Hollywood Movies Of The Decade

REGULATING AUDIENCES

14

Motion picture education

THE MOTION-PICTURE CRITIC

INCREDIBLE as it may seem, the motion-picture is still regarded as a scientific toy by the daily press. New York is supposed to set the pace for the entire country, yet what do we find? Of the regular dailies, but one is making an honest attempt to criticize current photodrama attractions. True enough, there appear columns of film notes, which are contributed by the publicity departments of the photoplay manufacturers, but anything resembling the regular dramatic department is practically unknown.

When a newspaper does review a photoplay it dispatches its regular dramatic critic. He may be a competent man in his own particular sphere, but when he tackles the motion picture he at once betrays his ignorance. He will say, for instance, that "The Love Chief" was "produced" at the Blank theater, whereas he should have written "presented." He is also fond of using the word "posed," when speaking of the actors. As any fan knows, once a photoplayer commences to pose, he is artificial. "Appeared" is a better word.

Speaking at a dinner in March, 1915, Arthur Brisbane, editor of the New York Evening Journal, said: "The success of the motion picture is based upon the stupidity and lack of intellectual development of the human race. I am one of the few living men who have never seen Mary Pickford or Charles Chaplin or Theda Bara or Miss Clarke. All I have seen is the 'Durbar' and Scott's South Pole pictures and 'Carmen,' which I couldn't escape because it was given in Mr. Hearst's house and I happened to be a guest there." When a great editor, such as Mr. Brisbane, permits prejudice to outweigh all other considerations, we begin to understand the apathy displayed by many newspaper editors toward the photoplay.

About two years before this speech was made, a well-known Chicago dramatic critic boasted that he had never seen a photoplay and did not wish to. Another dramatic critic made a fool of himself at a trade dinner when he mentioned a perfect, one-reel photoplay which it had been his pleasure to see. Naturally, his listeners thought he alluded to the old Griffith-Biograph pictures. "Spartacus," he said, when asked the name. "A one-reeler?" queried his questioner. "You must have only seen the final reel!"

Why should not photoplays be criticized the same as stage productions? The popularity of the feature photoplay, and the resulting improvements effected in the producing end, entitle the silent drama to be judged on a plane by itself. Why should a review be hidden among the "legitimate" stuff and criticized from the angle of a speaking play? It is not fair to the public or the producer. The newspapers claim that the average photoplay is not worth criticizing the story is too improbable to begin with. Let us grant that they are correct in their assumption. What is the critic for? Is it not his duty to dissect the faults and show how they may be remedied? Very well. He should be pleased because there is some useful work ahead of him. The producer has been accustomed to taking things easy because his efforts are sent out into the world without rebuffs. He may obtain a few "roasts" from the trade papers, but these do not reach the public at large, so why should he worry? Once a newspaper engages a motion-picture critic, he will put the producers on their mettle.

The motion-picture critic has difficulties which he alone can appreciate. There are something like one hundred productions, of all lengths and descriptions, released weekly. To see the entire output would keep the critic more than busy during each of the seven days. Then, there are space considerations. Under such conditions as exist in the big city it would not be advisable to just take the features playing at the leading theaters in the business and shopping sections, for the many ordinary shows situated in various other parts of the town and suburbs would be missed entirely. The only fair way is a middle course. It will be presumed that the critic keeps in touch with the latest output, which knowledge should greatly assist him to decide which are the best six or twelve productions of the week, and these should be included on his viewing schedule. This was the policy adopted by Wid Gunning, when motion-picture critic of the New York *Evening Mail* and proved satisfactory in two ways. It prevented readers from seeing a lemon and was an incentive for manufacturers to turn out better productions.

The duties of the small town motion-picture critic are considerably restricted. There are probably but two or three theaters in his territory, and all that is necessary is to review the star attraction of each house. If the theaters favor the daily change, as most do, it is impossible to review the features in time to be of service to the reader. For this reason I am inclined to the opinion that the small-town newspaper is best served by a syndicate service.

Where will the successful motion-picture critics come from? Many will be recruited from the photoplay-writing ranks because the first-hand experience thus gained will have taught them the qualities which go to the making of the perfect photoplay.

SHOWING OLD FILMS TO CHILDREN

The motion picture exhibitor is evidently under the impression that solving the child problem is solved by setting aside special matinees, but while this is a step in the right direction, it is far from satisfactory.

On the seven evenings weekly that the exhibitor solicits the patronage of adults, he generally presents the best of the latest productions. At the special children's performance, however, he seems to take a pride in showing motion pictures anywhere from a year old and up. This "junk," as it is termed in trade circles, is what is standing in the way of an adequate supply of new juvenile subjects. The exhibitor rents these films at the rate of one dollar per reel for one day from the exchange. Each reel the exchange has purchased from the producer for $100, so, in order to recover the initial outlay, two years must elapse before the exhibitor can obtain same at his price.

The exhibitor avers that the children's performance is not a paying proposition, but he is not going the right way to make it so when he puts on a cheap program.

He also considers that anything will do for the kiddies. There is a marked difference in the photoplays released several years ago and the present-day output. Now, wholesome stories, good acting, careful staging and attention to detail are the order of the day, and to feed children on an antiquated motion-picture diet is a penny-wise and pound-foolish policy.

Then, there are the educational subjects to be considered. Some of these are of timely interest when first shown, yet, by the time they are exhibited at the average children's performance, their instructive qualities are practically nil.

A child who has been taken to an ordinary performance will find many desirable qualities lacking in the children's performance, which will, in all probability, become a bore. He may then attend the photoplay theater without the parents' consent when undesirable (to him) pictures are on the program.

I realize that there is the exhibitor's case to be heard, but were he to charge, say, five cents additional, I feel sure that parents would not resent such an increase if it meant the newest juvenile productions being shown.

It is useless to appeal to the producer, who is a business man and must be guided by the needs of the exhibitor the retailer. The exhibitor must, therefore, be approached before any response can be made to the increased production of these pictures.

The problem, in my opinion, will only be solved when companies that specialize in the production of child photoplays are formed, and a chain of theaters opened all over the country catering to young folk only. But until this time comes it is up to the mothers to leave no stone unturned to persuade exhibitors to forsake their present cheap policy.

***

source: Dench, Ernest Alfred, *Motion picture education.* Cincinnati : The Standard publishing company, c. 1917.

Motion Picture Education

By

ERNEST A. DENCH

Author of "Making the Movies," "Playwriting for the Cinema," "Advertising by Motion Pictures"

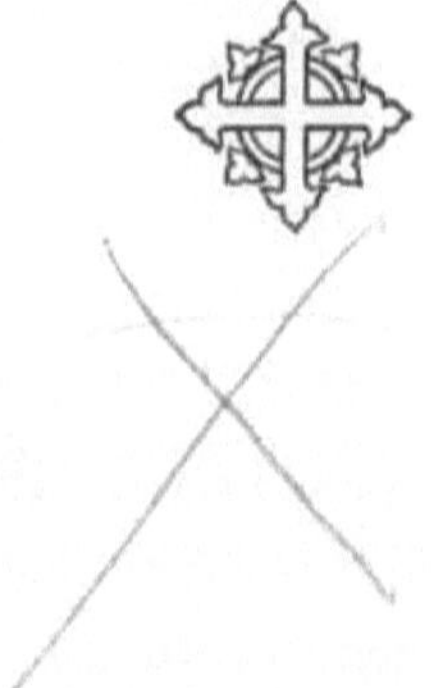

CINCINNATI

THE STANDARD PUBLISHING COMPANY

15

The Cinema : Its Present and Future

The Cinema: Its Present Position and Future Possibilities (1917) *is a report and summary of evidence taken by the Cinema Commission instituted by the National Council of Public Morals in UK. The NCPM was "deeply concerned with the influence of the cinematograph, especially upon young people, with the possibilities of its development and with its adaptation to national educational purposes" and the report includes several passages taken from interviews with children where commission members asked them questions about their cinema-going habits. This document is a thorough investigation into the cinema in 1910's Britain and what its effects might be on the viewing public. The report was favourable towards the film industry, which was delighted to receive such vindication of its work, and recommended the implementation of a system of official censorship, superseding that of local authorities. This rare document is strongly recommend it to anyone interested in early British film or the social history of film.*

IV.— THE VALUE OF THE PICTURE HOUSE

We are convinced that the picture house means so much happiness not only to children but even to adults living and working under adverse conditions, that any attempt at suppression would be a grievous social loss, and that, accordingly, every effort should be made to make all picture houses, as places of public amusement for old and young, clean and safe morally without sacrificing their interest and attraction. The testimony of one whose work for many years has been among the poor must be given. " In my judgment," says Mr. Massey, " it would be a great blow to my neighbourhood if the cinemas were suppressed or closed against the children. Just imagine what the cinemas mean to tens of thousands of poor kiddies herded together in one room — to families living in one house, six or eight families under .the same roof. For a few hours at the picture house at the corner, they can find breathing space, warmth, music (the more the better) and the pictures, where they can have a real laugh, a cheer and sometimes a shout. Who can measure the effect on their spirits and body ? To be able to make the poor, pinched-faced, half-clad and half-nourished boys and girls in the crowded slums in cities forget their pain and misery and their sad lot is a great thing, and the pictures do it." There is also the relief to the mother. " My knowledge," says the Rev. T. Home, "is of tired-out mothers working hard during the greater part of the day. They are only too glad to know that their children are able to go to an interesting entertainment such as the cinema, and that they are enjoying themselves out of the dangers and risks of the street."

Another social worker, less favourable to the cinemas on the whole, recognises that it is better for the children in her district to be in the picture house than even in their homes or in the street. This is a form of amusement that reaches a poorer class than any other, and it is, therefore, incumbent on those more favourably placed, while doing all possible to improve it, not to do anything that would rob shadowed lives of the little brightness that comes to them.

MORAL AND SOCIAL ASPECTS

The Alternatives to the Picture House

We must recognise that the picture house fulfils a useful and needful function amid social conditions which press very hard not only on the very poor, but even on the bulk of the working classes. So unsatisfactory is housing both in town and country, that there are few homes in which the leisure hours can be spent in quiet comfort and enjoyment. Not only are the slums and mean streets physically injurious, but they are beset with moral perils ; the sights seen and the sounds heard are potent factors in the deterioration of the morals and the manners of youth. For many months, owing to our climate, the parks and open spaces cannot supply a refuge from the house or the street.

Apart from the picture house the only resort that is offered to the teeming masses above the prohibited ages is the public house, with its constant temptation of strong drink and its no less polluted moral atmosphere.

The Influence of the Picture House in decreasing Hooliganism

Evidence has been submitted to us that the picture house has had some influence in reducing hooliganism, and in withdrawing custom from public-houses. " In my opinion," says Mr. Barnett, " the closing of the picture houses, or their prohibition to children, would have most unbeneficial results. In many cases the cinemas are the only form of healthy recreation available, and this is particularly the case during the long winter months. The children in question have neither the taste nor the facilities for indulging in any sport, and if the cinemas were closed to them, so far from the condition of the streets being improved, I am convinced there would be an immediate and immense increase in hooliganism, shoplifting and similar street misdemeanours. Fifteen years ago street hooligan gangs were a real menace and problem. Now such gangs are quite unknown in my district.

This opinion is confirmed by other evidence submitted to us.

The Cinema as a Counter-attraction to the Public-House

The same witness declares : "I think it is obvious that the cinemas are a strong counter-attraction to the public-house." All the witnesses questioned agreed with this opinion.

"The public-house proprietors", says Mr. Massey, "have made a complaint that the picture palaces have interfered with the takings, and one man told me that he lost from £15 to £20 a week." It must be observed that no picture house has a licence to sell intoxicating drinks, and no pass-out checks are given as in the theatre. It reveals a deplorable condition in many districts that in the opinion of some social workers even the least desirable picture house is a better place for the children than their homes or the streets, and that no thoroughly wholesome entertainment is being provided for them, especially in winter. While we have had sufficient evidence to show that there is need of much improvement as regards many picture houses, yet it is cheering to find that in the judgment of some of our witnesses there has been a marked improvement. The Rev. T. Home, who has known the industry from its very commencement, is confident that there has been a great improvement, and that there will be a still greater. He, in answer to a question, also expressed his conviction that the organised trades of the cinema industry. I will in reasonable time deal with anything that is undesirable. This view is confirmed by the Rev. A. Tildsley, who has watched the growth of the industry from its beginning, and rejoices in the improvement that has been made.

FINDINGS

1. While we recognise that there are difficulties in securing the necessary improvement, we do not admit that these are insuperable. Improvement is imperative.

2. While the charges of indecency have been greatly exaggerated and the evil is not nearly as widespread as is often assumed, yet that it does exist must be admitted, but not to any greater extent than in any other places of popular resort; and the regulations in force in London to suppress it should be made of general application.

3. Not only should the local authority enforce existing regulations, and regulations which after due inquiry and conference may be added, but the public should assist the local authority by calling attention to any disregard of them, or any acts of indecency.

4. A much stricter censorship than at one period prevailed is necessary. Steps have now been' taken to effect this improvement. The censorship should include not only films, but also the posters advertising the films.

5. Owing to the large number of children visiting the picture houses, special care is necessary to protect them from what would be morally, as well as mentally or physically, injurious to them.

6. The charge that the children are induced to steal in order to pay for admission cannot be regarded as a condemnation of he picture house itself, for (a) the same objection might be, and as been, offered to any object of desire or form of pleasure that powerfully affected the child; (b) even if the money stolen is spent in the picture house, it must not be concluded that the money was stolen for that purpose, and it is found that such money is used for other enjoyments; (c) it must also be recognised that the picture house is often used as an excuse, when it is not the reason for the theft.

7. Regarding the connection of the cinema with imitative juvenile crime, there was presented to us conflicting evidence — some

asserting as emphatically as others denied any general connection. Our conclusion is that such a connection does exist, though to a limited extent. It is not, however, a necessary connection, and not exclusive of many other factors too often ignored, because less obvious to the untrained observer of social phenomena.

8. Apart from "sex" and "crime" films, an injurious effect is produced on young minds by the excessive sensationalism and frightfulness of some of the films shown, and the wrong ideas of life and conduct often suggested.

9. It is evident that additional provision should be made for the young, both as regards arranging special exhibitions for them and securing suitable films to be there exhibited.

10. Despite the practical difficulties in making such provision, we urge that educational authorities and societies interested in the welfare of youth should co-operate in the endeavor to meet the need.

11. Compelled as we were in our inquiry to give special attention to the alleged defects in the picture house, we have been convinced by the amount of testimony offered in its favour of its value as a cheap amusement for the masses, for parents as well as children, especially as regards its influence in decreasing hooliganism and as a counter-attraction to the public-house.

12. The abolition of the picture house, as advocated by some, is impossible, even if it were desirable, as in our judgment it is not. On the other hand, we are strongly of opinion that not only is improvement practicable, but also of great national importance.

***

source : National Council of Public Morals. Cinema Commission of Inquiry. "The cinema: its resent position and future possibilities : being the report of and chief evidence taken by the cinema

Commission of Inquiry instituted by the National Council of Public Morals." London : Williams and Norgate, 1917.

The Cinema

Its Present Position and Future Possibilities

(Being the Report of and chief evidence taken by the Cinema Commission of Inquiry, instituted by *The National Council of Public Morals*)

CONTENTS

This volume gives a careful survey of a mass of evidence submitted by many experts—the Manufacturers, the Owners of Halls, Managers, Hygienists, Sociologists, Educationalists, Religious Leaders and Workers, Members of the medical profession, Students of juvenile psychology. A considerable amount of information upon the history and evolution of cinematography and its commercial development is included in this evidence. A very close and searching analysis of the moral, social, and educational significance of the "Picture Palace" is given ; and the results of many keen cross-examinations as to the tendencies and possibilities—dangerous or educative, good or bad—are skilfully presented.

The Report, findings, recommendations of the Commission, drawn up with scrupulous care, cover every aspect of the subject.

As a document on a live and up-to-date subject of vast and growing importance in its future relations to the moral, social, and educational welfare of the people, and especially of the young, this Report is of outstanding value.

LONDON : WILLIAMS AND NORGATE

16

Entertaining Hospital Patients by Film

It must be a trying ordeal for active folks to be bedridden, and consequently shut off from the outside world. No patient feels in a fit condition to undertake the necessary mental work involved in reading ; he wants this done for him, and the motion picture ably performs this service. By the photoplay he can be taken through the realms of romance and forget his pains and troubles for the time being.

The Ohio State Hospital at Massillon runs photoplay entertainments in the sick rooms for the patients, and other hospitals are gradually falling into line. These hints may prove of value to the hospital about to inaugurate such plays. The first item of importance is the projection machine, the cost of which ranges from $250 to $300. The authorities in various parts of the country insist upon the projection machine being enclosed in a fireproof booth, for if there is an outbreak of fire it cannot possibly spread further. Here an expense of $65 is involved. This booth, made of galvanized iron, gives the operator plenty of room in which to work, and being shipped in parts, the whole is easily set up with nuts and bolts.

Carbons are necessary to run the projector. These cost from $17 to $44, although prices vary according to market conditions. The next important link is the screen. Formerly a tablecloth or bed sheet was used, but science has now brought out many different screens, the best costing about one dollar and a half a foot.

Without music, motion pictures are divested of much of their charm, and while an orchestra of several pieces is best, one can get along satisfactorily with a piano.

If there is a man on the staff of employees who is well versed in electricity, he could easily become an expert operator. If he is the right sort of man he will not object to doing two or three hours overtime of an evening, or perhaps his hours at regular work can be curtailed.

There remains one last item, the light by which to throw the pictures on the screen. If the hospital has a power plant, the current from that can be used. Have the operator focus the projection machine exactly in the middle of the screen, not an inch to the right or left, or an inch above or below. If this is not attended to, no matter in what advantageous position a spectator sits, he will either have to hold his head up high or the players in the picture appear unnaturally long and slim. The rays of light take a straight path, and if they are compelled to turn aside, a peculiar, annoying effect is produced.

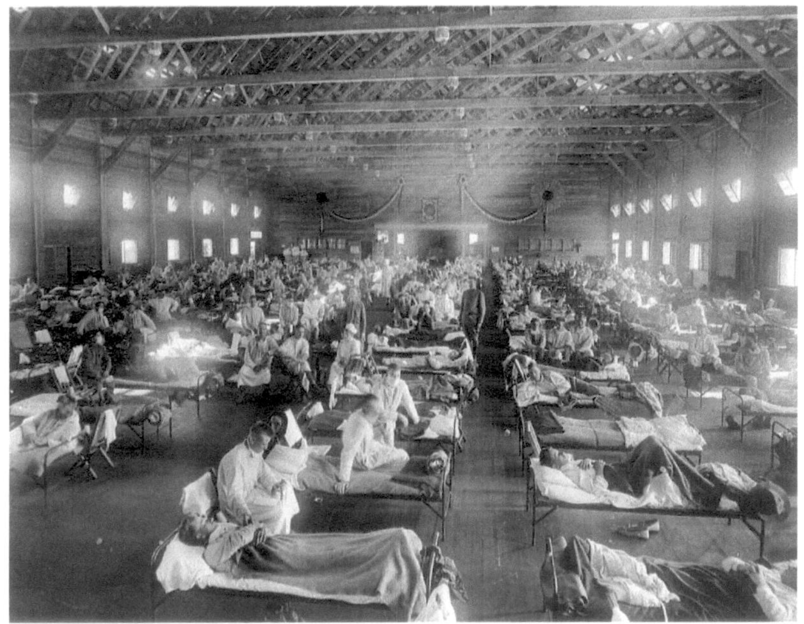

In selecting a suitable lens, the size of the room, the make of the projection machine, the length and height of the screen and the distance from the operating booth to the screen must be taken into consideration. It is false economy to purchase a cheap lens.

The standard speed at which pictures are projected is sixteen "frames" to the second. There are sixteen of these "frames," otherwise tiny pictures, to each foot of film, and a reel takes about eighteen minutes to unspool. If the projection is faster, things in the film move at a rapid, mechanical pace, while explanatory matter is snatched off before it can be grasped.

The operator will have to be provided with a tool outfit, which should include cement for mending broken films, a file for sharpening carbons, lugs, reels and machine oil.

The three chief distributing organizations, General, Mutual and Universal, operate a chain of exchanges throughout the country and between them release about one hundred productions weekly.

The producers marketing their wares under these factions receive ten cents per foot for each print they supply, .consequently every reel costs the exchange $100. It would be out of the question to show a film a single day on these terms, so it is hired out to the theaters booking them. The man who secures first-run service pays the highest price, but even then it only amounts to a part of the original price. As the age of a film increases, the rental decreases, until it can be hired for as low as one dollar per day. Even at this stage it is generally in good condition. The service has to be contracted for in advance, the films being shipped as required and re-shipped to the next theatre on the list at the expiration of the hiring term. It has been proven by experience that hospital patients appreciate comedy more than drama.

***

Source : Dench, Ernest A., "Entertaining Hospital Patients by Motion Pictures", *The American Journal of Nursing*, Volume 18, March 1918.

17

Regulating Film as an Entertainment

MOTION PICTURES AS A PHASE OF COMMERCIALIZED AMUSEMENT IN TOLEDO, OHIO (1919)

Reverend John J. Phelan's 1919 work, "Motion Pictures as a Phase of Commercialized Amusement in Toledo, Ohio," exemplifies a social survey driven more by moral concerns than social scientific inquiry. The book's title conveys a clear skepticism, which is reflected in the introduction's assertion that "there is a broad consensus among social science scholars on the need for community regulation of public commercialized entertainments." However, the study goes beyond mere critical suspicion of the public's movie preferences. Initially, Phelan acknowledges the positive aspects, outlining the significant benefits that motion pictures provide to society.

1. The providing of a reasonable-priced and highly entertaining form of amusement.

2. Convenience both as to accessibility and continuous play hours.

3. The promotion of family unity – as seen in attendance of the entire family.

4. The counteraction against the influence of the brothel, saloon, public dance hall and other questionable forms of amusement.

5. A provision for amusement and relaxation.

6. The supplying of information in regard to travel, history and world events.

7. The treatise of high moral and educational themes.

8. The movies as an "art."

While Phelan acknowledges that movies may attract those who are drawn to the abnormal, distorted, and often vicious aspects of life, he also believes in their potential for moral and educational value. What lends credibility to his study is his reliance on empirical data to support his views on motion pictures. Focusing on Toledo, Phelan details the number, types, sizes, locations, ownership, and functions of the town's cinemas in 1919, totaling six. He describes their proximity to other commercial amusements such as saloons and dance halls. He provides information on their value, rental fees, and the costs associated with machinery, fabric, employees, musicians, advertising, lighting, and heating. He presents data on audience demographics, ticket prices, and the structure of cinema programs. He also outlines the investment costs, operating expenses, and revenues of the cinema industry, offering valuable insights. Phelan includes evidence from studies conducted in schools, listing educational films that highlight the burgeoning sector of the film industry. He discusses moral concerns, censorship, and the struggle of "non-commercialized" amusements against the allure of cinema. Notably, Phelan concludes each book section with questions for "social studies" students, guiding them on what to inquire about in their own regions if they wish to conduct similar research on film audiences. The book ends with extensive appendices, featuring a useful bibliography, examples of pertinent legislation, a directory of Ohio cinemas with details on ownership, management, seating, location, and staff; sample questionnaires; excerpts of juvenile court testimonies; and more. Beyond the moralizing, the appendices provide a thorough overview of the cinema landscape.

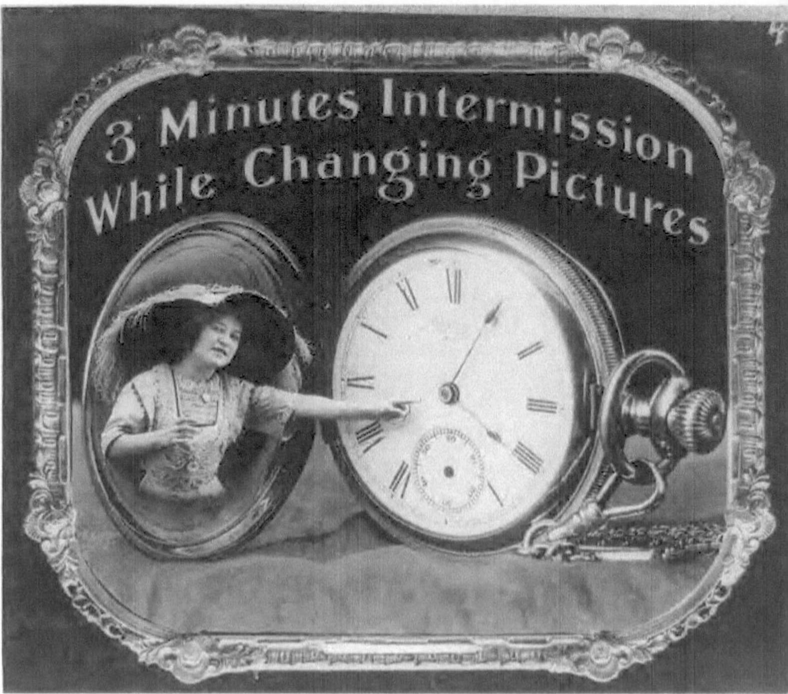

Positive paper print from lantern slide used in motion picture theaters as announcement. 1912. [Library of Congress]

FOREWORD

The writer is not opposed to Motion Pictures as a form of amusement. Pictures are possessed of infinite social and economic power and are capable of unlimited moral and educational worth. Hundreds of thousands each day secure their chief impressions of life, ethics, religion and morality thru the "movies."

Whether these impressions are beneficial — it is the special privilege of the mature and discriminating to judge. We surely cherish no desire to create standards of amusement for those best able to judge for themselves.

There is a large class, however, who do not exercise this nicely "discriminating" preference. In the cases when they would — they are handicapped by what is offered them. Statistics reveal that there are many who feed their nature upon the abnormal, distorted, suggestive and far too often, vicious things of life.

Students of social science are in quite general agreement as to the necessity of community control of public commercialized amusements. It lias been deemed necessary to place the motion picture industry under limited control in several States, and there is considerable agitation as to the necessity of a Federal Board of Censors for a more complete National control.

The social mind also is beginning to take notice of the great number of Juvenile Court cases: the newspaper reports concerning police arrests and the testimony of educators who deal with the young — as regards the increase of Juvenile delinquency. A prolific cause is the excessive and nondiscriminating patronage of picture houses.

It is poor policy, both moral and economic, for a community to allow its children to be filled with suggestions of filth and evil and then pay for it. Parents particularly must know that to tolerate or allow agencies to emphasize the dramatic value of the passions is a serious proposition. The "stress and strain" period of the adolescent child is most acute. Are we making the transition constructive or destructive?

The bedroom and lingerie style of drama are not constructive. Moving pictures with plots and themes fit only for a clinic cannot be tolerated in a democracy where children have a chance for growth and nurture. Our courts are practically crowded with a host of prematurely old — yet young persons in years. The placing of premiums on domestic infelicity denouments do not minimize the number of divorce cases, nor keep down the expense of operating police courts, infirmaries, hospitals and sanitariums.

We may excuse our responsibility toward the weaker members of society by graciously placing them in corrective and charitable institutions after they have "gone wrong," and cease all further care and thought of them, or, we may attempt by community measures and the exercise of a Christiansocial consciousness to check this increase of juvenile and adult delinquency at its source.

AN EXERCISE FOR ADVANCED SOCIAL STUDENTS.

A Questionnaire on Juvenile Standard for Motion Pictures.

Kindly give your careful consideration to each of the questions and prepare a written intelligent answer. They will form a basis for the selection of picture for children under 17.

It is understood that the emphasis in the selection of pictures for children, both those under 12 and those between 12 and 17 shall be placed on those themes and situations which are positive, helpful, constructive and inspiring. There is little need of statements of fundamental positions upon scenic, biographical, scientific, nature and industrial films. In the selection of amusing, dramatic and thrilling pictures, it is necessary that welldefined, sympathetic and comprehensive statements shall be formulated.

It is to be recognized that judgments will vary on individual pictures. This is inevitable because, for instance, of the swiftness of punishment, the repulsive nature of certain characters, the contrast presented, the lessons taught or the historic character of the acts, or persons involved.

It is important to distinguish, carefully, between pictures shown to children under 12 and boys and girls between 12 and 17. The mental outlook changes decidedly during the adolescent period.

None of these questions can be answered without consideration of possible exceptions. They have many individual qualifications which may modify decisions.

1. Are young people from 12 to 17 accustomed to repicture in their minds details secondary to the main story presented in the film?
2. Is it necessary that the moral be pointed, that evil be punished and good rewarded in dramatic pictures?
3. Please express your judgment of the value of pictures showing children doing wrong and subsequently being punished as a means of impressing a lesson. Do they learn the lesson or just remember the exciting adventures?
4. What position should be taken about the manifestations of love and lovemaking in its various forms before and after marriage?
5. Are there times when the causes and effects of unwise, indiscreet and overtrustful lovemaking snould be shown?
6. Are you committed to the policy of judging pictures for young people and children as a whole or in detail?
7. Can any rule be laid down refusing approval of pictures which play upon the weakness of any class or race?
8. Shall triangular and intricate problems of married life be shown under any conditions?

9. Shall crime and sex scenes which arouse unwholesome curiosity and stir the imagination be shown, be entirely eliminated or cut at the beginning of the questionable action?
10. Should Juvenile actors be encouraged to take adult parts?
11. Shall pictures be shown which make light of family ties, belittling the sanctity of marriage, presenting the humorous or serious deceptions of husband and wife?
12. What do you think of the use of action in motion pictures to arouse unthinking fear as a motive to check evil?
13. What is your opinion about scenes and pictures dealing with the underworld, its inhabitants, resorts and life?
14. Are you satisfied that clean pictures depicting action such as adventure, excitement, thrill, the work of detectives, cowboys, Indians, etc., should be shown ?
15. Have you any opinion about the portrayal of insane and feebleminded persons?
16. What is your feeling about the presentation of scenes in which persons appear partially clothed, in tights, bathing suits, etc.?
17. Is it possible to lay down any absolute rules about the use of weapons by the individual for defense or offence? Please try to formulate a statement.

***

Source :

- John Joseph Phelan, *Motion pictures as a phase of commercialized amusement in Toledo, Ohio*. Toledo : Little book press, 1919.
- Lessons from Toledo "The Bioscope", 2008 [with permission]

18

The Social Legislation of Motion Pictures

This rare book contains some of the recommendations from the National Board of Review of Motion Pictures for cuts to be made to some unnamed films. Donald Young, later professor of sociology at the University of Pennsylvania, was no admirer of this private organization which made censorship recommendations which were not legally binding and could be ignored locally. Young was the author of Motion Pictures: A Study in Social Legislation. Published in 1922, this PhD thesis must be one of the first doctorates to be awarded for the study of motion pictures.

Young's subject is the influence of motion pictures upon the American people, particularly children. As a piece of supposedly scientific social investigation it is remarkably partisan. It takes as read reports conducted by various groups with an interest in the morals of society which found motion pictures to be generally pernicious in their effects, and comes down on the side of legalized state censorship (by 1922 eight American states had instituted film censorship laws). A National Board of Censorship, later the National Board of Review, had been instituted in 1909, but its recommendations carried no legal weight. This is therefore not the social study that it claims to be, but rather an expression of fear, albeit one that is artfully and authoritatively expressed. Under the guide of social investigation, it looks for ways to control the medium whose malign tendencies are taken as a given.

The value of the text is firstly the period attitudes that it demonstrates, with the evidence that it calls on to support this. Secondly, it provides a rich picture of the various forms of municipal and state regulation that existed, their operations and aspirations. Thirdly, there are the several appendices with useful information, including the numbers of cinemas across America, state by state; figures for the importing of films from other countries; the rules of the British Board of Film Censors; the Standards of the Pennsylvania Board of Film Censors (the first US state to have censorship laws); and samples of eliminated scenes by the National Board of Review. [*The Bioscope*]

Positive paper print from lantern slide used in motion picture theaters as announcement. Each text superimposed on humorous photograph, and the whole shown in a fancy carved frame. [[US Library of Congress, Prints and Photographs Division]

A STUDY IN SOCIAL LEGISLATION

The motion picture industry is avowedly attempting to present the types of pictures which the audiences wish to see.

This is evidenced by the fact that the different types of houses show different types of pictures. For example, the motion picture houses are divided into two classes, the neighborhood houses and downtown houses. Neighborhood houses include all those which are in outlying parts of cities or in the smaller cities and villages. " Million dollar spectacles " are shown primarily in the downtown houses, i. e., those centrally located in large cities, because it has been found that if they are to be successful, such pictures must derive most of their income from the audiences which frequent the downtown houses. Many actors are known to be excellent drawing cards in the neighborhood theatre, while in the centrally located theatre, their pictures are failures. In reporting on the drawing ability of a picture, the exhibitor is usually asked to mention the type of audience to which it was shown. The president of one of the largest chains of theatres in this country remarked recently to the author that "the downtown audiences will stand for a lot more sex stuff than the neighborhood audience, and they expect it, too." We may safely say that the industry is trying to give its customers what they want, even though they may want questionable products.

CONFORMITY OF MOTION PICTURES TO THE ACCEPTED SOCIAL STANDARDS

During the one year period from the first of November, 1917, until the first of December, 1918, in the city of Chicago, in which city practically the same pictures are exhibited as in any other city in the United States, the acting censor deleted 55,604 feet of film from that submitted to him for approval, or a total of 974 subjects. The brief official statement of the reasons for the deletions is given in the following table, as is the relative frequency of their occurrence :

NUMBER OF CAUSES OF SUBJECTS ELIMINATION FT. DELETED (PER CENT.) :

- 467 Unlawful 31,040 47.9
- 220 Immoral 14,135 22.5
- 183 Indecent (Comedy) 6,539 18.77
- 42 Indecent (Drama) 1,978 4.2
- 36 . Nude 1,093 3.0

- 17 Obscene 400 1.7
- 6 Race 254 0.6
- 3 Creed 165 0.3

While the assigned causes of the eliminations are extremely vague, it is possible to see in them the previously mentioned sexual, property, personal, religious and state offenses. Combining the immoral, indecent (both in comedies and in dramas), nude and obscene, we find that over 50.0 per cent, of the offenses were against sexual standards. Offenses against race and creed are in a very small minority, as is to be expected from our previous analysis of standards. The term "unlawful" is the most vague of all. Still, although it has been impossible to obtain any exact statement of what is meant, it is not difficult to reach the conclusion that it refers to scenes that would be likely to incite unlawful acts through the portrayal of crimes and brutality. This heading includes most deleted subjects not included under the general heading of sexual offenses.

At that, it is a very close second, lacking only 3 percent, of being equal to the latter type of offense.

A committee of four hundred women from the Chicago Political Equality League presented the results of the most extensive, representative survey of motion pictures ever completed in the United States to the New York Biennial Convention of the General Federation of Women's Clubs. One thousand seven hundred and sixty-five plays were surveyed. About 21 percent of these were classed as bad, and nearly 30 percent, for example, showed criminal scenes. Only 20 percent were classed as being likely to have a positively beneficial effect on the audiences. The majority, or 80 percent, were either of a harmful nature or "not worthwhile."

Surveys similar to those made by the Chicago Political Equality League were made by Members of the Women's Federation in Michigan, Arkansas, South Dakota, West Virginia, New York, and Rhode Island. These were made on plans based on the methods used by the Illinois organization. Mrs. Bessie Leach Priddy, Chairman of the Federation's Department of Civics in 1919 is authority for the statement that these latter investigations "practically corroborated" the previous findings. It is, therefore, unnecessary to quote from material that, gathered under very nearly the same conditions as the Illinois material, leads to identical conclusions.

Number of plays under observation (1765 100%) NO / PER CENT.

- classed as good 348 / 20
- classed as bad 367 / 21
- "Not worth while" 1040 / 59
- plays showing domestic infelicity 282 / 16
- clandestine appointments 229 / 13
- drinking or bar room scenes 485 / 27
- scenes suggesting criminal acts 588
- gambling scenes 210 / 12
- lewd actions 193 / 11
- objectionable close-up filming 158
- risque or immoral scenes 229 / 13
- tending to create contempt for law, etc. 123 / 7
- contribute to delinquency 353 / 20

A survey of sixty-two motion picture houses in Minneapolis in September 1920, by the Women's Co-Operative Alliance while not so extensive as that by the Women's Federation, is probably more accurate and reliable in that it was completed by two workers who were acquainted with the methods of previous surveys, such as that by the Chicago Political Equality League, and who had used all possible precautions to standardize their judgments.

The features that the Federation considered objectionable were elaborated upon. A comparative study of their judgments later showed that they had been reasonably successful in reducing the personal element to a minimum. Since, however, their investigation was of an intensive rather than an extensive nature, its results cannot be considered representative or of any great value in a general discussion of motion pictures unless discussed from the point of view of their agreement with other material of a more general nature. In other words, so limited a sample may fairly be used only in conjunction with other samples.

Although made about five years after the Illinois survey, a noteworthy correlation is readily observable between the results obtained by the two investigations. The Illinois study found that 27 percent of the plays showed drinking or barroom scenes; the Minneapolis study found that in 19 percent of the plays that came under their observation, there were objectionable drinking or barroom scenes. The former found that 9 percent contained objectionable close-up scenes; the latter found 12 percent contained objectionable close-up filming. The former found that 11 percent showed lewd actions; the latter found 12 percent to be the corresponding figure for this item. Other items are possibly not entirely comparable due to the investigators' different working bases. It is sufficiently evident, however, even to the casual observer that there is no significant inconsistency between the two reports.

The above quoted examples of investigations of motion pictures confirm not only each other in their conclusions, but also bear out numerous less pretentious investigations and a large amount of the individual criticism which has been directed at the industry for the admitted purpose of many of its members of giving the people the things they believe they want, irrespective of the social effects of such a course of action.

PERCENT. DID THE PLAYS SHOW (YES / NO)

- Habit-forming drug using made attractive 4 96
- Objectionable bed-room scenes 4 96
- Criminal methods in a way to give instructive ideas. . . 6 94
- Prolonged objectionable love scenes 6 94
- Gambling made alluring or attractive 8 92
- Race friction 9 91
- Any objectionable close-up filming 12 88
- Any risque or lewd actions 12 88
- Religion or law ridiculed or held in contempt 12 88
- Any irreverence depicted 14 86
- Suggestive or objectionable exposure of person 16 84
- Gruesome subjects or death scenes, objectionable 16 84
- Objectionable drinking or bar room scenes 19 84
- Infidelity or disregard of marriage vows 20 80
- Underworld scenes or objectionable dancing 24 76
- Any obscenity, immorality or vulgarity 36 65
- Any sex problem handled in an objectionable manner 8 92

[...] It is perhaps worthy of noting that the investigations that have been considered are not representative of those against which much well-directed criticism has been aimed on account of the haphazard method of procedure and the use of questionable standards of conduct as the basis on which the judgments were built. An example of this type, which may be entirely accurate but is nevertheless inconclusive and likely to raise suspicions of bias, is one which was brought to the attention of the Committee on Education of the House of Representatives at its hearings on House Bill 456 for the creation of a federal motion picture commission, in 1916, by Doctor W. F. Crafts, superintendent of the International Reform Bureau. According to Doctor Crafts a state superintendent of schools of West Virginia studied the "real character of current motion pictures, " and found that 25 per cent, of the pictures were "good" and "not bad", and that 75 per cent, were bad" and "very bad." Cigarettes were shown in 35 percent, drinking in 50 percent, and gunplay and murder in 50 percent. "Deceit, intrigue, jealousy, or treachery was a leading feature in at least 40 per cent, of the programs presented."

Following the results of the surveys that we have reviewed, we may say without exaggeration that approximately 20 percent of the films shown in this country tend at least in part, to have a harmful effect if moving picture audiences are in any way influenced by that which is continually put before them. The fact that possibly 50 percent of the motion picture films will likely have some beneficial effect does not prove that the harmful plays should be disregarded. Violations of standards of conduct, which must, like things, result in similar conduct, are frequent under existing conditions, more frequent than is necessary, as has been shown by the fact that boards of censorship have eliminated many in the districts where legal provision is made for such work. Considerable weight must be given to the peculiar circumstance that the motion picture industry, one of the largest manufacturing industries in the country, has not fought facts with facts. No adequate refutation of the results of the various investigations has ever been offered.

Until present conditions are altered, it cannot be offered. The industry cannot afford to become entangled in an argument in which its members would be compelled to argue against their personal beliefs and the facts to show that their choice of plays, the result of a box office policy, is not, in a large percentage of cases, contrary to the accepted social standards.

Sources :

- House of Representatives, *Hearings before the Committee on Education*, January 13, 1916, p. 9.

- Women's Co-Operative Alliance, Inc., *Better Movie Movement*, Publication No. 38, Minneapolis, Minn., February, 1921.

- Donald Young, "Motion Pictures: A Study in Social Legislation". Doctoral thesis. Philadelphia, Pa. : Printed by Westbrook Publishing Co., 1922.

- The Bioscope [with permission]

A SOCIOLOGY OF EARLY AUDIENCES

19

Studying Audiences

"Viele Grüsse aus dem Union-Theater, Berlin, Alexanderplatz. Grösste und vornehmste Tonbild-Bühne der Welt"

Zander & Labisch, Photogr., Berlin W; 1909 (Union-Theater, 1909 eingerichtet im Grand-Hotel, Alexanderplatz 5-7)

Studying Audiences

The manager will learn much about his show by watching his patrons as they come out. It is not necessary to inquire what they think of the show. Comments will pass among them, which may be overheard by the manager and by the cashier as they pass the ticket window, commenting favorably and unfavorably upon the film pictures that they have seen a few minutes before. In this manner the manager may learn when any particular picture has favorable comment, and may endeavor to have his film exchange supply more of the same class; likewise, when any picture has a flood of unfavorable comment among the theatergoers themselves, the manager may try to influence his film exchange to avoid sending him that class of subject.

The words, "try to influence his film exchange," are chosen carefully to express the true position of the exhibitor, or theater manager, in the matter of obtaining film pictures acceptable to his patrons. The film exchanges as a rule take all the film pictures produced by the particular manufacturers from whom they buy. All of these film reels look alike to the film exchange man, and he would like to send them indiscriminately to his customers, to the exhibitors, or to theater managers. The service the theater manager will get, therefore, will be "hit or miss" of the film exchange stock of reels unless the manager uses some influence to govern the classes of pictures furnished him. Film exchanges are notoriously lax in the matter of selecting pictures for particular theaters. If the film service is to be what the manager desires, the deliveries of the film exchange must be watched constantly and carefully.

The manager who has learned the tastes of his audience should consider their tastes a requirement for obtaining the preferred classes of pictures from his film exchange. The audience's responsiveness in the theater is one barometer of public approval; the attitude and conduct of patrons leaving the theater is another. The ticket sales will be another, but this last is not so quick in its response indications.

When a picture pleases the audience, it may be the specific picture, or it may be the general class to which the picture belongs; in one neighborhood, dramatic and scenic may please more than comic or historical; in another nothing but comics can draw the crowds and send them away smiling.

The Program. Whether vaudeville is advisable and profitable, whether the song is a drawing card, or whether the audience would rather have solid pictures, all may be learned from watching the house during the performance and the faces and comments of the patrons as they pass out after seeing the performance. The choice of a program is an excellent factor in determining the theater's competitive position. There is little expense difference between a three-reel program, two reels, and a song.

***

source : David S. Hulfish, *Cyclopedia of motion-picture work a general reference work*. Chicago: American Technical Society Press, 1911.

20

A Sociology of the Cinema : the Audience

Extract from Emilie Altenloh, *Zur Soziologie des Kino: Die Kino-Unternehmung und die Sozialen Schichten Ihrer Besucher*, translated in part (by Kathleen Cross) as 'A Sociology of the Cinema: the Audience', *Screen*, vol. 42 no. 3, Autumn 2001, p.249-293 [with permission of Screen]. Emilie Altenloh's *Zur Soziologie des Kino: Die Kino-Unternehmung und die Sozialen Schichten Ihrer Besucher* (A Sociology of the Cinema) (1914) is one of the earliest scholarly theses on cinema and continues to be highly regarded today. Emilie Kiep Altenloh (1888-1985) was a German politician and economist with a strong interest in social welfare. Her study of cinemagoers in Mannheim, Germany, has gained recognition in recent years, partly because her exploration of the social factors driving cinema's popularity aligns with contemporary interests, and partly due to a growing focus on cinema as a social space in general. Between 1912 and 1913, Altenloh conducted a study of cinemagoers in Mannheim, which included a questionnaire sent to 2,400 individuals asking about their gender, age, social status, marital status, employment, religious beliefs, political affiliations, and filmgoing habits. Altenloh's methodology and findings remain significant for cinema historians. Her published study is divided into two parts, focusing on production and audiences. It includes very little information from the completed questionnaires, with the exception of an entry from a fifteen-year-old machine fitter. The favorite films listed by respondents include, in order: an unknown film, *Um fremde Schuld – Eine Episode aus dem Leben* (Germany 1912), *Die keusche Susanna* (Germany 1911 – a one-reel synchronized sound film of the Jean Gilbert operetta, not a four-part film), and another unknown film, presumably based on the 1912 operetta *Die moderne Eva* by Victor Holländer and Jean Gilbert. It is noteworthy that the German publishing initiative KINtop republished Zur Soziologie des Kino in a collective volume entitled Emilie Altenloh: Zur Soziologie des Kino. Die Kino-Unternehmung und die sozialen Schichten ihrer Besucher. This new German edition, published in the KINtop Schriften 9 collection, was released by Stroemfeld publishers in Frankfurt and Basel in 2012.The volume includes 15 contemporary reviews of Altenloh's original book, as well as contributions from researchers such as Andrea Haller, Heide Schlüpmann, Gerd Roscher, Martin Loiperdinger, Christiane Eulig, and Uschi Rühle. The volume totals between 108 and 128 pages, offering a rich academic context around this pioneering study on the sociology of cinema. A new bilingual edition, both in French and English, edited by Frédéric Gimello-Mesplomb and Hilda Inderwildi, was published in 2025, with contributions of Marianne Beauviche, Renaud Guinaudeau, and Julian Hammer.

Methodology: data collection

The observations set out below have been gleaned with reference to specially conducted surveys. This study draws on statistics indicating the frequency of cinema visits in a fairly large industrial town during two months in the summer and two in the winter. These statistics were kindly made available by four theatre owners, and the similarity of their results made it possible to get an idea of the significance of cinemas in general. In addition, these sources were underpinned by a survey, undertaken in the same town, whose aim was to establish the connections between social grouping, entertainment and cultural interests. In order to ascertain the nature of people's interest in the cinema, the following questions were asked, some of which were answered verbally and some by filling out a questionnaire:

1. *Name or sex (of respondent)*
2. *Occupation*
3. *Father's occupation*
4. *How old are you*
5. *Where were you born*
6. *Which school do/did you attend*
7. *Do you go to the theatre, public lectures, concerts, variety shows?*
8. *What do you enjoy best?*
9. *Do you go to the cinema? How often?*
10. *On your own or with other people?*
11. *What prompts you to go to the cinema on each occasion?*
12. *When do you usually go to the cinema (day of week, time of day)?*
13. *Do you stay for the whole programme?*

14. *What kind of films do you like best (dramas, comedies, nature documentaries etc.)*
15. *Has anything made a lasting impression on you? What?*
16. *Has the cinema offered you any artistic insights?*

A total of 2400 responses were obtained. This was achieved by contacting the committees of various trade associations, as the aim was to include as large a percentage as possible from each social group. Some committees then put us in contact with individual members of their associations. Young people (fourteen to eighteen years old) were surveyed in vocational and trade schools, while workers were surveyed in person. The remaining occupations -artisans, clerical workers, engineers, students, officers, and so on - were sent the forms exclusively through their trade associations or specialist publications. This yielded little success out of a total of 15,000 forms distributed, only about 200 were returned. With these groups, information had to be gathered in a different way, and personal impressions were incorporated to a greater extent than elsewhere in characterizing relationships to the cinema.

Generally speaking, for this latter group it can be assumed that judging the level of interest in cinema showings and the frequency of cinema visits solely on the basis of the completed questionnaires would be misleading. Among those surveyed through the trade associations, those who never went to the cinema generally put the form to one side with no further thought so that almost no forms were received from non-cinemagoers. This assumption is further strengthened by comments to this effect made by members of the associations surveyed. Numerical comparisons between the trades and other social groups are therefore impossible. In the case of laborers, however, as well as all the women surveyed, the results are more complete and allow for internal comparison. Answers were obtained in each case from all the members of the groups gathered specifically for the survey, enabling conclusions to be formed about the group as a whole. A similar situation holds for the results from the elementary schools, further education schools and trade schools, where all individuals in particular classes were included in the survey.

Most comprehensive, finally, are the results from one commercial further education school, gained by surveying all fifty-five classes with a total of 1381 pupils of both sexes. Attendance at this school is compulsory for all male and female apprentices of commercial trades. The school is organized based on a three-year attendance period, so that the first class is attended mainly by fourteen-to-fifteen-year-olds. The second is mainly by fifteen-to-sixteen-year-olds and the third by sixteen-to-seventeen-year-olds. In addition there are special classes for those who have obtained their one-year certificate from a middle school. This section of the survey includes all young people of a particular sort, categorized according to age. Due to the completeness of this part of the survey, analysis in this case will include a more detailed discussion of particularities and deviations from the overall picture, since these may be seen not as coincidental failings of the sample surveys but can be numerically adjusted, and assessed for their significance. Given the great expansion of trade in the town selected, all young entrants to the major occupations have been included. This is especially useful for cinema statistics because more money is generally spent on entertainment - and on the cinema in particular - during the years between when a young person starts to bring in a wage and when they get married than is spent later, something that is especially true in the case of young shop assistants. This is clearly demonstrated when this group is compared with members of other occupational classes (even if no account is taken of the fact that, of these latter, only those who show most interest in the cinema are included in the survey).

In order to be able to assess how significant cinema is for a town's population, it is crucial to ascertain whether it represents the only -or virtually the only - means of entertainment available, or whether other pastimes occupy the audience's time and capture their attention. There therefore follows a brief overview of other forms of entertainment in Mannheim, such as theatre and concerts.

Until 1908 there were no independent cinemas in Mannheim. People's desire for spectacle was satisfied by the Hoftheater, or court theatre, a second larger theatre and three speciality theatres. Occasionally, at a fair or some other popular festival, a traveling picture-show might exhibit the odd film, usually of a fairly poor technical standard. For the less well-off classes the court theatre was hardly an option - and indeed less so than today, when popular theatre productions with cheap seats provide at least a thinly spun thread between the theatre and those in the lower social classes who are particularly interested in it. General trends in the development of the modern stage suggest a further reason why most of the population has become alienated from the theatre. These trends are a result of the social divisions that have arisen alongside the contemporary organization of economic life. Most people are integrated into the overall economic system like a small cog in a machine, and this system not only dominates people's working lives but also constrains the totality of the individual. The free, inviolable sphere within which a person has sovereign control has been reduced to a minimum. This kind of life produces individuals defined primarily through the work they do, who find it very difficult to look for new avenues of development outside the sphere of life in which they find themselves. The ways in which people from different social groups seek to be entertained and have fun display certain characteristic features, and there is little understanding of what goes on outside one's own circles, let alone a sense of working together or of communal enjoyment.

In contrast to this highly constrained group is a comparatively small elite whose more favourable external circumstances have allowed them to retain a greater degree of inner freedom. These people are far removed from the majority in their whole way of feeling and thinking. For them, such manifestations of intellectual life as books and works of art do not remain external objects. Instead, they draw them into themselves and render them a living and integral part of their personality It is through this continual assimilation that the elite become bearers of the entire culture, and in turn determine its content.

This one-sided development is especially clearly revealed in modern theatre, whose entire repertoire can be divided into three groups. Firstly, there is modern drama, in which all the action is transferred onto the protagonists' inner life. The drama lies in the processes of highlighting and solving purely psychological conflicts. Nowadays this type of drama is cultivated at the best theatres, which have almost the character of private gatherings. It is here that members of this intellectual elite seek intellectual nourishment with their more finely-tuned emotional life, they alone are in a position to understand the playwright. Alongside these are the classical dramas. However, since the average person today is rooted more than ever in the present and has proper understanding only of contemporary problems and issues, he is less drawn, purely in terms of human sensibility, to things classical and indeed often lacks the level of understanding required for forming a judgment from an artistic point of view, since this is only possible with a certain cultivation of taste. The third type is opera, which has numerous adherents from all social circles and constitutes the very essence of theatre for broad sections of the population today. Modern comedies and operettas in particular continue to attract large audiences, and have been staged in Mannheim from time to time over the past few years in response to an urgent need for light entertainment. Most of the big concerts of the season take place in the three auditona of the town's concert building. Variety shows and cinemas, of course, also provide entertainment. What is more, they draw away from the theatre all those whose principal concern is to spend a few hours being entertained. Finally, the various cycles of lecture series should be mentioned, which on different evenings of the week during the winter are a source of fascination for some sections of the population. They might, therefore, have the effect of diverting them from the cinema.

This was the situation regarding pleasure and entertainment facilities in the town when the cinema movement entered dramatically onto the scene in 1908. Although emanating from the urban centers, cinema also made its presence felt in provincial towns. In both locations, the same process occurred first the audience's attention was diverted from similar entertainment forms, variety shows and cabarets. But new options awaken new needs, and thus the number of cinemas has grown far beyond the number of cognate establishments. The trend in Berlin typifies this, where in addition to the thirty-four variety theatres that existed in 1908, another 300 cinemas have since sprung up. Typically, this trend did not emerge immediately after the new invention became well known, but only when sensations-drama or sensational drama brought a radical change to film representation and when the picture houses were transformed from dimly-lit, confined spaces into luxurious and comfortably furnished buildings. These two factors have proved decisive for the role played by the cinema today.

From that point onwards in its development, cinema won over ever more elevated social groups and became, as it were, 'presentable'. At first, cinemagoers traveled incognito and were actually somewhat embarrassed if their predilection became public knowledge. Times have moved on, for today a screening of *Der Andere/ The Other*, with Albert Bassermann in the leading role, constitutes a society event. The modern city-dweller nowadays considers the phenomenon of cinema as something perfectly natural, and an occasional visit to the cinema is just as much a part of life as taking afternoon tea at five on the Kurfurstendamm.

The same development has been repeated on a smaller scale in provincial towns, including Mannheim As has already been noted, two out of three variety theatres have disappeared, one of these was converted to a cinema, and eleven additional cinemas were built from scratch. Five of these are located in the town centre and seven more around the edge of town. Most of them have only come into existence during the past three years. Their location is also a key feature. Until 1910 only four movie theatres existed in the town centre and one in the town's suburbs. At that time there was as yet no appreciable difference between them. In terms of both their external appearance and the content of their screenings, they were all tailored to the most primitive expectations. Accordingly, the audience was almost exclusively recruited from the lower social groups. Then the cinemas began to spread rapidly In Mannheim this involved three new cinemas being opened in 1910 and three more in 1911. These theatres are by no means all located in the town centre, but rather in those parts of town where the largest section of the contemporary cinema audience lives, namely the labourers. At the same time, two film theatres in the town centre began to differentiate themselves by the more elegant design of their audition, the introduction of more expensive seats, and by employing a small ensemble of musicians instead of an orchestra or solo piano player The location and interior design of movie theatres, then, as well as the ticket price, are more significant in determining the composition of the audience than the quality of what is being shown. Hence the opening in 1912 of a competitor establishment, the third of this more luxurious group.

The same phenomenon that had occurred some years earlier in Berlin was now being repeated here, cinema became a fashion, indeed different social circles became actively involved in supporting and promoting it. A demonstration screening was organized by the Verein der Kunstler und Kunstfreunde (Association of Artists and Friends of the Arts), in which the peculiar pictorial effects made possible through cinematography were shown, using extracts from various films as examples. These illustrations did not provide a model for producing good film programs so much as an education in an artistic way of viewing: the emphasis was not on the material content of the film but solely on the effect of individual images and movements. In practice only very few film directors have as yet shown any interest in achieving an image in which the succession of moving bodies forms a continuous whole with the background of a scene in order to create a harmonious aesthetic impression In film, however, when such an impression is achieved, all attention becomes focused solely on film's potential as a series of images, with action and plot neglected. Thus a degree of perfection is achieved, but only ever in one aspect of film presentation

Similarly, and despite all efforts, there has never existed, even in theory, the movie theatre with a perfect programme. Any judgments that might be made concerning the excellence or quality of any given enterprise can therefore be of only limited significance. The three town center theatres mentioned above, which incidentally are owned by rather large theatre chains, in contrast to the private enterprises of the suburbs, differ from the smaller ones mainly in terms of their external appearance. At least the worst excesses have been eradicated from the program, partly out of consideration for the reputation of the enterprise, and in their place, nature documentaries have come to constitute a somewhat larger part of the repertoire.

The remaining cinemas, usually situated at various locations in the suburbs, differ from one another in only a few minor respects, the most important being the quality of ventilation in the auditona. They offer everything that those seeking horror and sensationalism could possibly want, and appeal to the type of person vilified in many quarters as pernicious and lacking in taste. Loud, garish posters with sensational titles, often specially altered to appeal to a particularly unshockable audience, cover entire facades. Just how low the level is and what kind of visitor is expected is best summed up by the following notice in one of the auditorial "Wrecking of chairs and benches is prohibited'. Anyone who has ever strolled through the suburbs knows this kind of den. Each is no better and no worse than the other and is. In the end, always tailored to the needs of audiences who remain shockingly indifferent to, and uncritical of, the entertainment they enjoy, as long as what they are watching does not require any intellectual effort.

Taken together, the twelve cinemas [in Mannheim] offer about 4500 seats for a population of around 204,000. A certain degree of saturation appears to have been reached with this figure, and further theatre openings would be unlikely to be profitable. The proportion of cinemas to inhabitants is similar in a number of other industrial towns But cinemas have already achieved such widespread popularity that all other forms of entertainment lag far behind. One cinema (albeit one of the largest) has as many visitors every evening as the court theatre Based on an estimated number of seats and on statistics from all the different theatres, it can be concluded that around 7500 people go to the cinema every evening. By contrast, even when all the other entertainment establishments are counted together and when, for example, several events are taking place at the same time, audience figures still do not equate with those for cinema.

The number of cinemagoers on particular days of the week seems to be subject to certain regularities. This is clearly demonstrated by a curve whose shape varies according to whether the cinema is located in the centre or in working-class areas of town. In the case of the former, the minimum frequency falls with greatest regularity on a Friday. The reason for this is not immediately apparent. Perhaps we need to postulate a psychology of the different days of the week in order to explain it. Fridays represent a kind of preparation, a time of waiting for events that will occur on the free Saturday afternoon and Sunday, which are usually devoted exclusively to the pursuit of pleasure. Fridays have always been largely devoted to work, perhaps precisely in order to increase the sense of anticipation for the coming days of rest Saturday itself, on the other hand, is almost already a part of Sunday, especially since the introduction of earlier closing times. One practical reason could also be the fact that Friday has traditionally been cleaning day in multi-roomed apartments, when the women of the petite bourgeoisie and middle classes are busy with domestic duties: these women make up a large proportion of the cinema audience, especially in the film theatres under consideration here.

The curve for the frequency of cinema attendance in the suburbs shows that the minimum falls on Thursdays, when money has probably already become a little tight, whereas on Friday, pay day, the frequency picks up again The majority of visitors to these cinemas are laborers, that is people who have to manage with limited means and who have usually spent their weekly wage by Thursday. For the majority, however, going to the cinema seems to be the Sunday outing For those who are busy at work during the week, going to the cinema is the only time when they are completely freed from the daily grind. All other forms of entertainment are more expensive (for instance, the theatre) or more difficult to arrange (as is the case with plays). But picture houses can be found in every part of town So on Sundays all the cinemas are reserved for those sections of the audience who only have time to go on that day Moreover, both the suburban establishments and the bourgeois cinemas in the town centre show a three- to fourfold increase in audience numbers on Sundays compared with weekdays After all, everyone likes to be seen out in their Sunday best, so people will happily pay a little extra for the greater comfort provided by the better theatres. On the remaining days of the week, cinema attendance manifests fewer but also fairly regular fluctuations.

The relationship between day of the week and cinema attendance is the only factor that has a consistent impact on the shape of the curve No other factor seems capable of disrupting this regular cinema attendance not the weather, nor well-attended events happening at the same time in the theatre or the Rosengarten, nor even the festival weeks of I to 12 May or special entertainment programs. At most these circumstances have the effect of increasing or reducing the level of cinema attendance in one instance or another within the frequency shown on each day of the week.

This is true first and foremost for particular programmes. But it is only in isolated instances that any of the above influences can be identified at all In the absence of any other decisive factors the likely reason why extraordinarily large numbers of people go to the cinema on some days may be rainy weather. Boredom and inactivity soon set in, and for many that is just the right mood for a trip to the cinema. What also emerges from the questionnaires is that bad weather in itself can be a reason for going to the cinema. But those who are thus motivated do not constitute the majority. Even if the odd rainy day does not always mean a particular increase in cinemagoing, business does fall off greatly during the summer months, which explains the large number of bankruptcies during the warm season.

It is easy to see why the theatre and concerts do not exert much influence on attendance figures when one considers that two cinema establishments alone have, almost without exception, more visitors daily than the court theatre and the Rosengarten put together - and there are twelve cinemas in town. Generally speaking, a person will rarely have any trouble choosing between the theatre or the cinema, because each suits a completely different mood. This is even more true where concerts are concerned: thus these too exert no diversionary influence. For example, within a given two-month period, the greatest number of cinema visits occurred at the same time as three well-attended concerts in the Rosengarten Public lectures on science pose still less of a challenge to the cinemas. The obvious inference is that the cinema audience is recruited from different circles than the audience for other events. Where individuals are strongly influenced by a lively interest in things musical or scientific, the lure of cinema seems to be less enticing. But wherein lies the great attraction that still guarantees it a sizeable following. By what means has cinema gained an audience that at one time was completely indifferent to any kind of artistic representation? Let it be remembered that one cannot watch a film drama while sitting at a table drinking beer, for example, as one can a variety number, or as one might elsewhere enjoy the "Indian Nightingales' or some peasant band from the Schhersee as background entertainment. And how does the cinema win for itself an ever-increasing audience from among the educated classes ?

We shall first consider some general reasons for the above before going on to consider films which have proven particularly appealing to audiences Whenever the question is raised as to why cinemagoing is on the increase, the answer usually given is, 'The admission price is low, and you can go anytime without making any special preparations' The strongly sensual nature of most films, intensified by the accompanying music as well as the darkness of the cinema auditorium, is also emphasized as exerting appeal. This certainly represents part of cinema's mysterious power of attraction. But these factors can only have an effect when they act in concert with many other causes, products of the general character of our times which influence the audience in particular ways.

The low admission charge certainly plays an important role For someone of modest means there is, after all, a difference between spending seventy-five pfennigs on the most uncomfortable seat in the theatre and occupying a box in the cinema for considerably less However, as the questionnaires show, almost one third of cinemagoers, including those from less well-off social groups, go to the cinema once or even several times a week, and therefore spend just as much money on entertainment as they would on a once or twice-monthly trip to the theatre, a fact that substantially undermines this line of argument. The second reason holds more water-namely, the fact that going to the cinema is possible at any time one chooses. What seems to me more crucial, however, is that both the cinema and those who visit it are typical products of our times, that characterized by constant preoccupation and a state of nervous restlessness. Those who are constantly on the go at work during the day can not even free themselves from this haste when they want to relax.

As they pass the cinema they will go in to seek some distraction for a short period of time and, as they do so, will already be half thinking of how they might fill the next few hours In order to connect with a work of art, whether it be drama, a piece of music or a painting, a certain amount of time and leisure is required, as is a focusing of the mind. Cinema does not demand such concentration It creates such powerful effects that even shattered nerves can be stirred to life, and the rapid succession of events, the jumble of the most varied kinds of things, allow no room for boredom.

But it is not only the fast-paced, overwhelming form of cinema (which is indeed its very element) that satisfies so completely the needs of a broad mass of people: the content of cinematic representations also does this. The fact that erotic films and films about criminals attract such large audiences is utterly explicable' surely these films are the only ones that can strike a chord among the mass of people whose intellectual life is often in deep slumber and who have nothing in common with each another, at least as far as more elevated matters are concerned. As Heine wrote of that mode of understanding that is founded on the common basis of inferior emotions. "Rarely have you understood me, rarely too have I understood you, but whenever we found ourselves in the mire, we understood one another straight away".

Alongside these particular attractions there is another possible reason for cinema's great popularity. Cinema drama has stepped in where theatrical literature has left a gap. Nowadays, dramas are not at all popular and yet they are exactly what a large part of the audience is looking for and appears to have found in the cinemas. Plenty of action, lively changes of scene these are the main characteristics of cinema drama, and those who seek such excitement come here at their own expense. The particular suitability of cinematic technique has placed cinema drama on this path and earned it its popularity. Objection might be raised at this point that historical and classical theatre dramas are just as rich in observable action. This is why they are still the most popular, relatively speaking, because people understand them But in general the current generation is not especially interested in history, and the social problems of today are much more of a lively presence in people's lives. The same themes provide the basis for most film dramas. Here they are dealt with not in abstract form, but through real examples and in the most powerful possible form. Whether or not what is shown has artistic integrity is not at issue here, the point is that cinema moves with the current of the times, it is the product of a general sensibility. In a certain sense, people's interest in printed news and weekly reports in the cinema is not so different from their interest in cinema drama. Certainly one major reason for this is their devotion to and immersion in the present. Film drama enters and touches people's everyday lives. It might be that extraordinary. Which way this trend will go we cannot yet predict; but it will certainly be in stark contrast to modern theatrical literature.

The features that characterize cinema drama have already been named, and the more pronounced these typical features are the more they captivate the audience. If one looks at those programs that have proven especially popular, this success can usually be traced to particular dramas. For example, the Asta Nielsen dramas were without exception the most popular ones shown in the better theatres (In contrast, the situation in the suburbs was exactly the opposite. For the film *Zu Tode gehetzt / Harried to Death*, with Asta Nielsen in the lead role, audience numbers fell below average). A programme containing the hit *In der Nacht des Urwalds / Jungle Nights* had almost the same high frequency of attendance, as this film is named again and again on the questionnaires.

All these box-office successes (they include, along with the Asta Nielsen dramas, *Das Weib ohne Herz / The Heartless Woman, Abgnmde / Abyss* and *Fraulein Frau / Little Miss Woman*) have certain uniform features in common. Dramas made by German companies, exclusively, are at the centre of interest. It is true that most of the great dramas that are shown originate from German-based companies, simply because these can in general be sold somewhat more cheaply. Furthermore, a degree of conformity to national tastes seems to be the most favourable precondition for great success in terms of the kinds of films shown. In the case of the majority of cinemagoers, one cannot yet speak of a cosmopolitan sensibility in people's tastes. Films that allow members of an audience to make a connection with their own social environment, whether depicting life as it is or as they wish it could be, are the most popular and allow for greater emotional identification. Indeed emotional identification really is the crucial factor here, for film representations have a very direct effect, sweeping spectators along with the action and enabling them to experience the hero's predicaments. Foreign films are less able to arouse this sort of interest because they are characterized by a foreign sensibility and only seldom strike a chord.

In terms of their content, all the films deal with that issue which constitutes the object of representation not just in film but in every area of art nowadays, and it is this theme that gives rise to their popularity in the first instance. Social issues are the focal point of attention. These dramas usually describe a woman's struggle between her natural, sensual instincts and the social conditions she faces that contradict these instincts. Her options are either spinsterhood on the one hand or the possibility of marriage to a husband who usually comes from a significantly higher or lower social group on the other. The details of the action, such as the strong sensual content of individual scenes to which the material frequently lends itself, do not miss their mark and are the reason why these films are especially popular. These kinds of drama are so significant for cinemas and so popular within individual occupational groups that we have already addressed above the question of their overall role in the cinema. The following chapter sets out, however, to examine in greater detail their relationship within and towards the cinema movement as a whole. [...]

Sources :

1. Emilie Altenloh, *Zur Soziologie des Kino - Die Kino-Unternehmung une die sozialen Schichten ihrer Besucher*, Andrea Haller, Martin Loiperdinger, Heide Schlüpmann (Eds.), Frankfurt am Main : Stroemfeld Verlag, coll. Kintop Schriften, 2007.
2. Emilie Altenloh, *Zur Soziologie des Kino: Die Kino-Unternehmung und die Sozialen Schichten Ihrer Besucher*, translated in part (by Kathleen Cross) as 'A Sociology of the Cinema: the Audience', *Screen*, vol. 42 no. 3, Autumn 2001, p.249-293.
3. Emilie Altenloh, "A Sociology of the Cinema: The Audience". I: Simpsons, Philip, Utterson, Andrew og Shepherdson, K.J. (red.) (2004), *Film Theory: Critical Concepts in Media and Cultural Studies, volume III*. London: Routledge.
4. McCormick, Richard W. og Alison Guenther-Pal (red.) (2004), *German Essays on Film*. New York: The Continuum International Publishing Group Inc.

5. Luke McKernan (11. august 2012) *A sociology of the cinema* [Internet], The Bioscope : http://thebioscope.net/2012/08/11/a-sociology-of-the-cinema/ [Lest 25. may 2024]
6. Frédéric Gimello-Mesplomb and Hilda Inderwildi (eds.). Emilie Altenloh: On the Sociology of Cinema: The Cinema Enterprise and the Social Classes of Its Visitors. London - New York : OpenCulture Academic Publishing, 2025

Dr. Emilie Kiep-Altenloh at a reception in the 1960s
(credits : Hamburg State Archives)

21

How Workingmen spend their spare time

How many people writing on early film know about this? Using a bit of lateral searching on the Internet Archive, I found *How workingmen spend their time*, a doctoral thesis by one George Esdras Bevans, submitted at Columbia University in 1913. I've not come across it before, and it seems few film histories refer to it, yet it is a marvellous source of information on cinema-going, audience leisure tastes, and the relationship of earnings and work-time to leisure, with a wide range of evidence demonstrating the prime position of cinema in the public mind just before the First World War.

Here's the author's description of his methodology:

This investigation has been undertaken in order to determine how workingmen spend their leisure hours. On the suggestion of Dr. Franklin H. Giddings, Professor of Sociology, Columbia University, the questionnaire method was adopted and a time schedule prepared. The investigation was begun in February, 1912. More than 4,000 schedules were distributed among workingmen thru the agency of Labor Unions, Clubs and Churches; but altho much interest in the study was manifested, only 113 properly filled out schedules were returned, and these were considered too few in number to serve as a basis for any general conclusions. In the Fall of 1912 the Bureau of Social Service of the Home Mission Board of the Presbyterian Church became interested in the study and agreed to engage investigators to interview workingmen in order to secure a sufficient number willing to answer the questions. This investigation began on November 1st, 1912, and was completed on February 3rd, 1913. Schedules to the number of 868 were returned by the paid investigators. In addition 31 schedules were obtained as the result of a Workingmen's Mass Meeting held November 12th, 1912, at the Labor Temple, 14th Street and 2nd Avenue, New York City. By February 3rd, 1913, 1,012 schedules had been secured from New York City, 10 from Rochester, N.Y., and 5 from Utica, N.Y. After the tabulation had been partly completed 43 schedules were received from other cities and were used in the closing part of the study relating to Expenditure of Money. Altogether, 1,070 schedules were returned, and these serve as a basis for the present study.

Bevans then goes into great detail, describing the processes he took, the particular statistical method employed, and the resistance that he sometimes received (questions were asked, "Who is back of the study?" "What capitalistic scheme is this?" "Why not investigate the employers and see how they spend their spare time?"). He also provides the questions asked and the forms supplied. The main body of the text is tables with accompanying analysis, under such headings as 'The Relation of Occupation to the use of Spare Time', 'The Relation of Wage to the Use of Spare Time', and 'What Men Usually Do on Certain Hours and During Certain Hours'. As an example, here's is one of the the tables accompanying the heading 'The Relation of Hours of Labor to the Use of Spare Time':

TABLE I ✓

Percentage of men who report time spent for various purposes during one week according to specified Hours of Labor.

	HOURS PER DAY			
	8—9	9—10	10—11	11 and over
Number of men	*289*	*257*	*128*	*132*
SOCIAL AND OTHER AGENCIES	%	%	%	%
Labor Union	39.4	24.8	16.4	8.3
Clubs or Lodges	58.1	44.7	35.9	26.5
Church or Synagogue	51.9	51.0	52.3	50.0
Public Lectures	32.2	26.4	16.4	5.3
Art Galleries	8.7	7.7	3.9	.7
Library	14.5	15.1	10.1	2.2
Private Study	16.3	14.3	14.8	3.0
Night School	6.2	10.8	9.4	3.0
Motion Pictures	55.0	63.0	64.0	57.5
Theatres	56.7	44.3	39.0	24.2
Dance	25.0	14.3	13.2	9.0
Saloon	31.1	31.1	32.8	28.7
Pool	14.9	10.1	13.2	8.3
Cards	37.0	30.7	36.7	44.6
With Family	82.0	76.2	78.1	81.0
Newspaper	96.2	93.3	92.1	78.7
Magazine	31.1	22.5	15.6	19.6
Books	40.8	33.0	22.6	17.4
Friends	78.9	79.7	79.6	67.4

This isn't the place to go into a detailed analysis of the data, but essentially one finds that whatever the working man's circumstances, his hours of work or his earnings, the motion picture was the favoured way of spending one's spare time. This might be expected, but it is invaluable to see the assumption tested against other leisure options, the availability of free time, and the means to pay for it. Here's a table on the relationship of age to spare time:

TABLE 15

Percentage of men who report time spent for various purposes during one week according to specified Age Group.

	17—24 years	25—35 years	36—45 years	46 yrs. and over
Number of men	*207*	*331*	*187*	*82*
SOCIAL AND OTHER AGENCIES	%	%	%	%
Labor Union	15.9	25.3	33.1	45.1
Clubs or Lodges	48.3	40.1	44.9	51.2
Church or Synagogue	39.1	45.3	62.5	69.5
Public Lectures	28.0	26.5	17.1	14.6
Art Galleries	9.6	6.6	5.3	3.6
Library	20.7	11.7	3.7	7.3
Private Study	26.0	10.8	6.4	3.6
Night School	17.8	6.6	1.6	......
Motion Pictures	43.9	65.2	48.1	46.3
Theatres	63.2	45.9	31.0	28.0
Dance	37.6	16.3	6.4	1.2
Saloon	17.8	32.6	42.7	30.4
Pool	25.1	12.3	2.6	2.4
Cards	25.6	39.8	41.7	26.8
With Family	65.7	80.3	94.6	85.3
Newspapers	94.6	90.3	89.8	92.6
Magazines	29.9	23.2	21.9	18.2
Books	45.8	26.8	27.8	20.7
Friends	81.6	80.0	71.6	65.8

OK, not everyone interested in silent cinema is going to be that engrossed by statistics, but the sociology of early cinema is still a grievously neglected subject, and if we don't relate the films to th people who saw them, its hard to say what we are doing investigating early films at all.

There were other such early sociological studies. The most notable is Emilie Altenoh's study of film audiences in Mannheim, Germany over 1912/13, published as *Zur Soziologie des Kino: Die Kino-Unternehmung und die Sozialen Schichten Ihrer Besucher* (1914), part translated as *A Sociology of the Cinema* in *Screen*, vol. 42 no. 3, Autumn 2001. I hear tale that a full translation into English is underway. Another is M.M. Davis' *The Exploitation of Pleasure: A Study of Commercial Recreation in New York City* (1911). There is always something a little unsettling about people being studied anatomically in this way – and generally working-class people. What seemed irrational or in need of explanation (and then control) by elites, seemed wholly rational to those enjoying the experience. But we still have to be glad that such studies were done. As Bevans' data amply proves, watching movies was, quite simply, a good way of spending your time.

Luke McKernan (august 2012).

***

source :

1. Luke McKernan (11. august 2012) *A sociology of the cinema* [Internet], The Bioscope : http://thebioscope.net/2012/08/11/a-sociology-of-the-cinema/ [Lest 25. may 2024] [with courtesy of Luke McKernan]
2. George Esdras Bevans, *How workingmen spend their time*, Ph.D. thesis, Columbia University, New York : Columbia University Press, 1913. Available on Archive.org.

HOW WORKINGMEN SPEND THEIR SPARE TIME

BY

GEORGE ESDRAS BEVANS, M. A.

Submitted in Partial Fulfillment of the Requirements for the Degree of Doctor of Philosophy in the Faculty of Political Science
Columbia University

NEW YORK
1913

22

The photoplay : A psychological study

Hugo Münsterberg (1863-1916), a German-American psychologist, published *The Photoplay: A Psychological Study* at a pivotal moment in his academic and personal career. Invited by William James to Harvard in 1892 to direct the psychology laboratory, he was a pioneer of applied psychology, constantly seeking to extend scientific methods to new domains. Published in 1916, just months before his sudden death during a conference at Radcliffe College, this work represents the first systematic study of cinema as an artistic form and psychological experience.In a context of personal and geopolitical tensions, Münsterberg, torn between his German origins and American adoption, was under significant pressure during World War I. His pro-German positions had led him to be suspected of espionage and marginalized by his Harvard colleagues. His study of cinema was part of a broader approach to applying experimental psychology to cultural phenomena, examining the perceptual and cognitive mechanisms of the spectator.His methodological approach offers an innovative analysis of cinematic perception's psychological processes, developing the hypothesis that cinema constitutes a new autonomous art form whose experience transcends physical reality. Münsterberg examines the mechanisms of identification with characters and the aesthetic dimension of the medium, making a decisive contribution to the emergence of cognitive film theory and anticipating future developments in psychology and film studies.

Everything so far has referred to the emotions of the persons in the play, but this cannot be sufficient. When we were interested in attention and memory we did not ask about the act of attention and memory in the persons of the play, but in the spectator, and we recognized that these mental activities and excitements in the audience were projected into the moving pictures. Just here was the center of our interest, because it showed that uniqueness of the means with which the photoplaywright can work. If we want to shape the question now in the same way, we ought to ask how it is with the emotions of the spectator. But then two different groups of cases must be distinguished. On the one side we have those emotions in which the feelings of the persons in the play are transmitted to our own soul. On the other side, we find those feelings with which we respond to the scenes in the play, feelings which may be entirely different, perhaps exactly opposite to those which the figures in the play express.

The first group is by far the larger one. Our imitation of the emotions which we see expressed brings vividness and affective tone into our grasping of the play's action. We sympathize with the sufferer and that means that the pain which he expresses becomes our own pain. We share the joy of the happy lover and the grief of the despondent mourner, we feel the indignation of the betrayed wife and the fear of the man in danger. The visual perception of the various forms of expression of these emotions fuses in our mind with the conscious awareness of the emotion expressed; we feel as if we were directly seeing and observing the emotion itself.

Moreover the idea awakens in us the appropriate reactions. The horror which we see makes us really shrink, the happiness which we witness makes us relax, the pain which we observe brings contractions in our muscles; and all the resulting sensations from muscles, joints, tendons, from skin and viscera, from blood circulation and breathing, give the color of living experience to the emotional reflection in our mind. It is obvious that for this leading group of emotions the relation of the pictures to the feelings of the persons in the play and to the feelings of the spectator is exactly the same. If we start from the emotions of the audience, we can say that the pain and the joy which the spectator feels are really projected to the screen, projected both into the portraits of the persons and into the pictures of the scenery and background into which the personal emotions radiate. The fundamental principle which we recognized for all the other mental states is accordingly no less efficient in the case of the spectator's emotions.

The analysis of the mind of the audience must lead, however, to that second group of emotions, those in which the spectator responds to the scenes on the film from the standpoint of his independent affective life. We see an overbearing pompous person who is filled with the emotion of solemnity, and yet he awakens in us the emotion of humor. We answer by our ridicule. We see the scoundrel who, in the melodramatic photoplay, is filled with fiendish malice, and yet we do not respond by imitating his emotion; we feel moral indignation toward his personality. We see the laughing, rejoicing child who, while he picks the berries from the edge of the precipice, is not aware that he must fall down if the hero does not snatch him back at the last moment. Of course, we feel the child's joy with him. Otherwise, we should not even understand his behavior, but we feel more strongly the fear and the horror of which the child himself does not know anything. The photoplaywrights have so far hardly ventured to project this second class of emotion, which the spectator superadds to the events, into the show on the screen. Only tentative suggestions can be found. The enthusiasm or disapproval or indignation of the spectator is sometimes released in the lights and shades and in the setting of the landscape. There are still rich possibilities along this line. The photoplay has hardly come to its own with regard to these secondary emotions. Here it has not emancipated itself sufficiently from the model of the stage. Those emotions arise, of course, in the audience of a theater too, but the dramatic stage cannot embody them. In the opera the orchestra may symbolize them. For the photoplay, which is not bound to the physical succession of events but gives us only the pictorial reflection, there is an unlimited field for the expression of these attitudes in ourselves.

But the wide expansion of this field and of the whole manifoldness of emotional possibilities in the moving pictures is not sufficiently characterized as long as we think only of the optical representation in the actual outer world. The camera men of the moving pictures have photographed the happenings of the world and all its wonders, have gone to the bottom of the sea and up to the clouds; they have surprised the beasts in the jungles and in the Arctic ice; they have dwelt with the lowest races and have captured the greatest men of our time: and they are always haunted by the fear that the supply of new sensations may be exhausted.

Curiously enough, they have so far ignored the fact that an inexhaustible wealth of new impressions is at their disposal, which has hardly been touched as yet. There is a material and a formal side to the pictures which we see in their rapid succession. The material side is controlled by the content of what is shown to us. But the formal side depends upon the outer conditions under which this content is exhibited. Even with ordinary photographs we are accustomed to discriminate between those in which every detail is very sharp and others, often much more artistic, in which everything looks somewhat misty and blurring and in which sharp outlines are avoided. We have this formal aspect, of course, still more prominently if we see the same landscape or the same person painted by a dozen different artists. Each one has his own style. Or, to point to another elementary factor, the same series of moving pictures may be given to us with a very slow or with a rapid turning of the crank. It is the same street scene, and yet in the one case everyone on the street seems leisurely to saunter along, while in the other case there is a general rush and hurry. Nothing is changed but the temporal form; and in going over from the sharp image to the blurring one, nothing is changed but a certain spatial form: the content remains the same.

As soon as we give any interest to this formal aspect of the presentation, we must recognize that the photoplaywright has here possibilities to which nothing corresponds in the world of the stage. Take the case that we want to produce an effect of trembling. We might use the pictures as the camera has taken them, sixteen in a second. But in reproducing them on the screen we change their order. After giving the first four pictures we go back to picture 3, then give 4, 5, 6, and return to 5, then 6, 7, 8, and go back to 7, and so on. Any other rhythm, of course, is equally possible. The effect is one which never occurs in nature and which could not be produced on the stage. The events for a moment go backward. A certain vibration goes through the world like the tremolo of the orchestra. Or we demand from our camera a still more complex service. We put the camera itself on a slightly rocking support and then every point must move in strange curves and every motion takes an uncanny whirling character. The content still remains the same as under normal conditions, but the changes in the formal presentation give to the mind of the spectator unusual sensations which produce a new shading of the emotional background.

Of course, impressions which come to our eye can at first awaken only sensations, and a sensation is not an emotion. But it is well known that in the view of modern physiological psychology our consciousness of the emotion itself is shaped and marked by the sensations which arise from our bodily organs. As soon as such abnormal visual impressions stream into our consciousness, our whole background of fusing bodily sensations becomes altered and new emotions seem to take hold of us. If we see on the screen a man hypnotized in the doctor's office, the patient himself may lie there with closed eyes, nothing in his features expressing his emotional setting and nothing radiating to us. But if now only the doctor and the patient remain unchanged and steady, while everything in the whole room begins at first to tremble and then to wave and to change its form more and more rapidly so that a feeling of dizziness comes over us and an uncanny, ghastly unnaturalness overcomes the whole surrounding of the hypnotized person, we ourselves become seized by the strange emotion. It is not worth while to go into further illustrations here, as this possibility of the camera work still belongs entirely to the future. It could not be otherwise as we remember that the whole moving picture play arose from the slavish imitation of the drama and began only slowly to find its own artistic methods. But there is no doubt that the formal changes of the pictorial presentation will be legion as soon as the photoartists give their attention to this neglected aspect.

The value of these formal changes for the expression of the emotions may become remarkable. The characteristic features of many an attitude and feeling which cannot be expressed without words today will then be aroused in the mind of the spectator through the subtle art of the camera.

THE FUNCTION OF THE PHOTOPLAY

Not only the news pictures and the scientific demonstrations but also the photoplays can lead young and old to ever new regions of knowledge. The curiosity and the imagination of the spectators will follow gladly. Yet, even in the intellectual sphere, the dangers must not be overlooked. They are not positive. It is not as in the moral sphere where the healthy moral impulse is checked by the sight of crimes that stir up antisocial desires. The danger is not that the pictures open insight into facts which ought not to be known. It is not the dangerous knowledge that must be avoided, but it is the trivializing influence of a steady contact with things that are not worth knowing. The larger part of the film literature of today is certainly harmful in this sense. The intellectual background of most photoplays is insipid. By telling the plot without the subtle motivation that the spoken word of the drama may bring, not only do the characters lose color, but all the scenes and situations are simplified to a degree that adjusts them to a thoughtless public and soon becomes intolerable to an intellectually trained spectator.

They force on the cultivated mind that feeling which musical persons experience in the musical comedies of the day. We hear the melodies constantly, feeling like we have heard them ever so often before. This lack of originality and inspiration is not necessary; it does not lie in the art form. Offenbach and Strauss and others have written musical comedies which are classical. Neither does it lie in the form of the photoplay that the story must be told in that insipid, flat, uninspired fashion. Nor is it necessary in order to reach the millions. To appeal to the intelligence does not mean to presuppose college education. Moreover, the differentiation has already begun. Just as the plays of Shaw or Ibsen address a different audience from that reached by the "Old Homestead" or "Ben Hur," we have already photoplays adapted to different types, and there is not the slightest reason to connect with the art of the screen an intellectual flabbiness. It would be no gain for intellectual culture if all the reasoning were confined to the so-called instructive pictures and the photoplays were served without any intellectual salt. On the contrary, the appeal of those strictly educational lessons may be less deep than the producers hope, because the untrained minds, especially of youth and of the uneducated audiences, have considerable difficulty in following the rapid flight of events when they occur in unfamiliar surroundings. The child grasps very little in seeing the happenings in a factory. The psychological and economic lesson may be rather wasted because the power of observation is not sufficiently developed and the assimilation proceeds too slowly. But it is quite different when a human interest stands behind it and connects the events in the photoplay.

The difficulties in the way of the right moral influence are still greater than in the intellectual field. Certainly it is not enough to have the villain punished in the last few pictures of the reel. If scenes of vice or crime are shown with all their lure and glamour the moral devastation of such a suggestive show is not undone by the appended social reaction. The misguided boys or girls feel sure that they would be successful enough not to be trapped. The mind through a mechanism which has been understood better and better by the psychologists in recent years suppresses the ideas which are contrary to the secret wishes and makes those ideas flourish by which those "subconscious" impulses are fulfilled. It is probably a strong exaggeration when a prominent criminologist recently claimed that "eighty-five per cent. of the juvenile crime which has been investigated has been found traceable either directly or indirectly to motion pictures which have shown on the screen how crimes could be committed." But certainly, as far as these demonstrations have worked havoc, their influence would not have been annihilated by a picturesque court scene in which the burglar is unsuccessful in misleading the jury. The true moral influence must come from the positive spirit of the play itself. Even the photodramatic lessons in temperance and piety will not rebuild a frivolous or corrupt or perverse community. The truly upbuilding play is not a dramatized sermon on morality and religion. There must be a moral wholesomeness in the whole setting, a moral atmosphere which is taken as a matter of course like fresh air and sunlight. An enthusiasm for the noble and uplifting, a belief in duty and discipline of the mind, a faith in ideals and eternal values must permeate the world of the screen. If it does, there is no crime and no heinous deed which the photoplay may not tell with frankness and sincerity. It is not necessary to deny evil and sin in order to strengthen the consciousness of eternal justice.

But the greatest mission which the photoplay may have in our community is that of aesthetic cultivation. No art reaches a larger audience daily, no aesthetic influence finds spectators in a more receptive frame of mind.

***

Source :

Hugo Münsterberg, *The photoplay : a psychological study*. New York, London : D. Appleton, 1916.

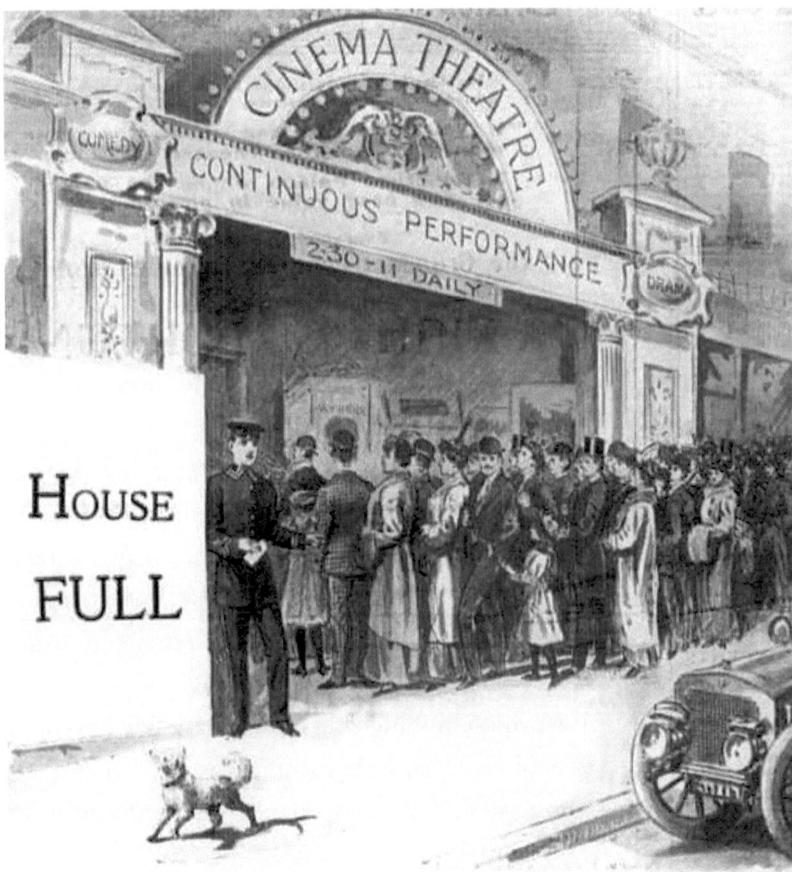

Advertisement for the Brixton Scala
Brixton Free Press, 1914

23

Psychology of the Cinema Audience

Students at the Majestic, Ann Arbor, Michigan, watching a movie (1913)
[courtesy of the Media History Digital Library & Archive.org]

The manufacturer of photoplays studies his audience through the box office. To him there are two kinds of audiences, the good and the small. He calls a given photoplay ninety-five percent perfect if ninety-five out of a hundred local exhibitors report good audiences on the particular day or week when the play was exhibited. But we as students or critics or serious minded photoplaywrights cannot afford to make hasty inferences from the mere facts of dollars and houses. If we are to improve the photoplay as art we need to penetrate more philosophically into the nature of the audience, we need to understand the experience of the average member of that audience, his reactions, sensations, feelings, and thoughts during the exhibition of a picture. As practical artists we must see our goal before we start, we must address our message before we send it. And we should know our audience before we attempt to communicate with it.

It must never be forgotten that the theatre audience is a crowd. A crowd is a compact mass of people neva together by a single purpose during any period of t.itne whether long or short. The various units are in close contact with each other, the crowd existing as such while this close contact is maintained. In the theâtre a particular crowd exists as such only during the time of the performance and can never exist again once it has been broken up after the particular performance for which it came together. The close contact is spiritual as well as physical. You not only touch elbows with your neighbour and live in his atmosphere but you are infected by his emotions and share his desires, purposes, reactions. This close contact gives the crowd a peculiar psychology. The individual in the crowd is not the same ias when alone. He is subconsciously influenced by his companions or neighbours until his emotions are heightened and his desire or ability to think is lowered. He laughs more easily and at less comic things in a crowd than when he is alone. In the crowd he is more responsive, more demonstrative, more kind, more cruel, more sentimental, more religious, more patriotic, more unreasoning, more gullible than when alone. A crowd, therefore, is more emotional and less intellectual than its members were before they came together.

While the crowd is single-minded the public is manyminded. The public may be looked upon as a vast web-like association of unified groups, families, cliques, coteries, leagues, clubs, and crowds. A crowd can never exist as such for more than three or four hours at a time, or while the close contact is maintained and the single interest is held. But a public may have space between its units and time between its sessions. Furthermore, the public is permanent in its existence. Its groups come in contact, though not simultaneously; views are exchanged, discussions are carried on, letters are written, until as a result of all this reflection a deliberate expression is arrived at. This deliberate expression is called public opinion.

But a crowd by its very nature never has time to reflect. It must decide and act on instinct or impulse or, at best, on the first flash of thought. After that crowd has been broken up, the individuals may upon reflection reverse their decisions. These second thoughts, these mature judgments may then become a part of public opinion. It happens, therefore, very often that political orators — we need mention no names — can sway crowds but cannot sway the public. It happens too that a play may be applauded by three or fifteen or fifty crowds and yet not finally make for itself a public. This is so because the crowd grasps at the obvious and immediate, because it is impressed by surface values. But a play cannot become a permanent possession of civilizatipn unless its values are deep, fundamental, vital, subtile, and permanent ; unless, in short, it will stand the test of study and time.

Classic stage plays such as Macbeth or The School for Scandal or Lady Windermere's Fan have stood this test and have their public, who will attend a performance whether done by college dramatic society, society amateurs, or the best professional talent And, through their masterpieces, dramatists like Shakespeare, Sheridan, Wilde, Shaw, Maeterlinck, and Barrie have their public, who will be interested in any play, no matter how obscure or inferior, attributed to these authors. But in the brief history of the photoplay no scenario writer has succeeded in winning a public. It is true that Mr. Griffith has a public ; but he is a director and producer as well as a writer. At present not one photoplay out of a hundred gets a public. The momentary nature of exhibition prevents it. Photoplays are seen and judged by single isolated crowds, in Boston and Kalamazoo and Galveston, but rarely by a steady succession of crowds in one place, a succession that might finally develop a public criticism. There are exceptions, of course, such as *The Birth of a Nation*, and *Intolerance*.

But in the motion picture world it is the "star", the actor or actress, who gets the public. Mary Pickford has her public. Francis Bushman has his. The Drews and Chaplin have theirs. Here again the conditions of exhibition are responsible. A play is flashed upon the screen, fades away, and dies with that performance. It lives again somewhere, perhaps in Brooklyn or Hoboken, but not for us. We cannot read it. Nor can we find it or see it again at will. It exists only for a crowd. The plays go; but the "stars" remain. In the same theatre we may applaud them again tomorrow or next week. They will exhibit their powers in a new story, a new "vehicle", but we give the "vehicle" casual attention, because we know that it, too, will be whisked away. Meanwhile we become familiar with the performers. We know their names, and ages, and favourite amusements. We criticize them. We tell our friends that they are not so wonderful as advertised to be, or that every one must be sure to see them. Thus under present conditions the interpreter, rather than the play, secures a firm grasp upon the public.

Yet these difficult conditions in the motion picture world need not discourage the cinema composer. If he can only capture enough crowds, say a thousand or more, he, too, will ultimately win a public, providing, of course, that the surface appeal which pleased the crowd will, when penetrated, reveal a deeper appeal capable of holding the public. But how can he coax even one crowd into captivity? The cinema composer studies the psychology of spectators in a motion picture theatre, he will discover that for them three classes of appeal exist in every film that telles a story. They are:

- first, the ***sense appeal*** to the eye;
- second, the ***emotional appeal***; and,
- third, the ***intellectual appeal***.

The sense appeal and emotional appeal are primary, elemental, and strong, while the intellectual appeal is secondary and relatively slight.

The visual sense of the spectator reacts first to the beauty of the subject photographed. Thus a moonlit lake, a surfswept beach, sprucecovered foothills, an Italian villa near a mountain pass, the interior of a richly furnished mansion — all give the eye a sensation of pleasure, a pleasure which is quite apart from their meaning, their relation to the plot of the play. The spectator might be too stupid to understand the story and yet might thoroughly enjoy the picture. This delight of the eye is a primitive sensation; yet it is experienced by every spectator whether he be an infant or a mature man of culture. It is more than an appreciation of a picture; it is a delight in the subject itself. The spectator easily imagines that he is in direct contact with the beautiful reality itself, and forgets that the camera has intervened.

The eye is especially pleased by certain types of physical movement which the motion picture can transmit, and which cannot be transmitted through any other art medium. When a pebble is thrown into a pool a number of circular ripples immediately take form and, expanding in concentric rings, finally flatten out and lose themselves in the still surface of the pool. The eye is pleased by these expanding ripples and by the endless multiplication of rings which rise mysteriously from the point where the pebble went down. The eye does not discover any particular meaning in this subject; it merely enjoys the abstract motion. If motion were absent, and the rings were still, as they would seem in an ordinary photograph, there would be no sense of visual pleasure. Other examples of pure motion pleasing to the eye are the pouring rush of a waterfall, the rhythmic undulations of the sea, the fan-like spreading of a sky rocket, the slow curling of smoke from a factory fimnel, the varying balance of a bird in flight, the steady forward thrust of a yacht under full sail. In all these subjects it is the continuous movement rather than the static moment which pleases the eye. And the motion picture is the new and unique medium through which these movements may be reproduced with artistic effect.

There is a keen pleasure of the eye also when appealing motion identifies itself with the expression of the human body, individually as in the case of a dancer, and en masse as in the case of a regiment on parade. This response of our senses to human form and physical movement is primary and elemental, and takes place before our brain has time to interpret the dramatic significance of the visible stimulus. Hence we see that a fundamental duty of the photoplaywright is to give the performers full scope for the physical appeal, and to set their action amid an environment which shall instantly impress the eye of the spectator. This first impression on the observer is tremendously important. And the scenario writer must remember that it is his business to furnish good subjects for the director, and that both he and the director must conspire with the photographer to captivate the eye of the audience, because whatever other appeals a photoplay is to make, it must first appeals to the eye.

While the spectator at a photoplay feels the visual or purely physical sensation described above, his spiritual experience is enriched by the emotions which are being kindled by the play. We have already said that the crowd is very highly susceptible to emotional appeal, that the individual in the crowd is more emotional than when alone. His emotional experience is of a twofold nature. He feels what we may call "self-emotion" or emotion which has no reference to any person in the play or to any other person in the world, and he feels a social emotion, a feeling of social relation with, and a personal interest in, the characters of the play. The *self-emotion* in the cinema theatre when viewing a pictured scene, is like the *self-emotion* in real life face to face with real nature. We have all experienced it, yet cannot easily describe it. Sometimes it may be a vague sense of longing as we look through the slender birches across a wide bay at the low majesty of the spruce-covered bank beyond. But the longing does not formulate itself. We do not know exactly what we want or feel. It is a mysterious mingling of contentment and sadness. In the same way the eternal whiteness of an Alpine peak, a dim sail on the far horizon, the luminous reflection of a summer cloud in a mountain lake — all stir in us an emotion of silent marvel or wonder or a vague longing for something — something beyond our present experience. Sometimes the *self-emotion* may be more naive, a thrill or excitement at some action or disturbance, at a street crowd rushing to a fight or a fire, even when we are not quite sure or do not really care what it is all about.

The sense of an incipient or impending stir outside us stimulates a corresponding agitation within us, and we are impressed before we really know what it is that has impressed us. The spectator in the motion picture theatre easily yields to these simple emotional appeals. He surrenders to the illusion of art, and easily imagines that he is in the presence of real nature or of the actual original action. But the spectator's emotional experience is still more vivid in his dramatic sympathy, his social interest in the characters on the screen. The fact that social emotions can be aroused by something which is confessedly not real, by mere pictures of people who do not exist except in imagination, is of fundamental importance in dramatic or literary art. This illusion makes drama a tremendous power. It makes our world very large and our human acquaintance very wide. Fiction becomes real. Fictitious characters become more real even than their authors. To us Shylock seems more real than Shakespeare. We could almost believe that the Jew was a historical figure and the Englishman. Don Quixote, Sherlock Holmes, and Peter Pan surely are more real than Cervantes, Conan Doyle, and Barrie. We know the characters of story so intimately because through the medium of art we have come in personal contact with them, have admired their powers, or sympathized with their joys and sorrows. In the motion picture theatre this illusion of personal contact with the characters is especially strong. We admire or dislike, love or hate, approve or disapprove, forgive or refuse to forgive, these mere shadows on the screen. We select our friends from among the heroes and heroines, but we scorn the villainous, the stupid, and the low. We weep real tears over sorrows which we know do not really exist. We applaud triumphs which we know are never really achieved. We have definite fears and dreads and hopes and ambitions for merely imaginary characters.

These social emotions arise in us, not only because we are sympathetically interested in the outcome of any human struggle, as we shall see in a later chapter, but because, by a law of psychology, we project our very selves into the characters on the screen. Thus every spectator in the audience may get by proxy the experiences and emotions of the character he is observing. The identification of self with fictitious characters is especially true of childhood. Lovers of Dickens will remember David Copperfield's statement that as a child his only and constant comfort was reading novels, putting himself into all the good characters and putting Mr. Murdstone, his hated stepfather, and Miss Murdstone into all the bad ones. In the theatre today the little girl identifies herself with the queen or with the adventuress. She imagines herself as magnificent as one and as clever as the other. The little boy identifies himself vividly with the hero in all his nobility or with the villain in all his shrewdness. It is human nature to crave an increasing experience, an experience which is not limited by the boundaries of circumstance, or propriety. Where actuality imprisons us, art sets us free. In art the janitor may become a king, the postman, a general; you may become a train robber, your sister, a vampire, and I may become a millionaire. Thus all of us may get vicariously the experience which we could not get or would not want in actual life.

An interesting representation of this projecting of self into a character may be found in the Blue Bird photoplay Undine. The film represents a man reading the story of Undine to his little girl. When they get to the part about the fisherman's child the little girl says to her father, "I want to be their little girl". The father gives her permission, and through the rest of the film we see the role of the fisherman's child played by the same girl who sat on her father's knee and listened to the reading of the story about that child.

One of the factors involved in our s)rmpathies with the characters on the stage or on the screen is the factor of the performer who plays the part. After having seen Sarah Bernhardt in Camille or David Warfield in The Music Master or John Barrymore in Justice we can never think of the chief characters in those plays respectively except in connection with the performers. A reading of the play in book form before or after it is acted does not make the stamp of the actor's personality any less indelible. In the case of the photoplay where the film version is the only one, the coalescence of the actor with the part he plays is even more complete. In fact it would be impossible for us to come in contact with the photoplay character at all except through the photographed pantomime of the performer. Therefore in the photoplay our social emotions toward the characters are largely conditioned by our like or dislike of the actor or actress.

In fact, the "movie fan" is quite content to admire acting apart from its significance in the interpretation of character. His eagerly surrendered dime is a tribute to the physical skill or daring of a fellow being, some comedian who rolls humorously down a flight of stairs, or some actress who leaps from a racing automobile to the cowcatcher of a train. This is an elemental and primitive emotion. For thousands of years gaping humanity has been thrilled by the juggler and the acrobat. And who of us has not inherited this savage appreciation ? Which of us does not some time steal away from the press of business, the depths of philosophy, or the heights of art to thrill at the gifts of the baseball pitcher, the prize fighter, or the cabaret dancer? Such admiration of physical skill in a fellow being is basic in all the appreciation we have for theatrical performance. Julia Marlowe and Charlie Chaplin, antipodal as they may seem, have built their success on the same foundation, this social emotion of the crowd, this admiration of physical ability in a fellow. The crowd by no means objects to welldeveloped characters in a play, but it demands that these characters shall be conceived or adjusted to reveal the powers of favourite actors or actresses. Any theatre crowd, except one composed of dramatists and critics, would rather see a first class actor in a second class play than a second class actor in a first class play. This emphasizes what we have already said, that the crowd grasps at the obvious and immediate, and is impressed by surface values. The actor is the surface value of the character he interprets. In the case of the good actor this surface value is an accurate index to the character which lies beneath. In the case of the bad actor the surface value is like a gaudy curtain which prevents our seeing the character created by the author. In either case the eye of the crowd feeds eagerly upon the show of the surface.

Here then is the moral. If the cinema composer wishes to arouse the social emotions of the crowd, if he wishes to give every spectator a personal escape into the fascinating region of vicarious experience, he must conceive and delineate his characters in the terms of the greatest acting values. The emotions of an audience are the treasure trove of the artist ; and for the time being the motion picture "star" is the only one who can unlock it.

The intellectual appeal of a photoplay is slight compared with its emotional appeal. The momentary, flashing nature of exhibition and the psychology of the crowd give the spectator little opportunity or desire to exercise his intellectual faculties. Yet he has certain intellectual experiences while seeing a photoplay. The fundamental one is the satisfaction of curiosity. We constantly desire new material to add to our store of knowledge. We crave novelty. The average American scans his newspaper with bated breath. But the recognition of a thing as new is an intellectual process. Our judgment declares a thing new by comparing it with the old which we already possess. Then the new itself becomes old and the adventure of the mind must begin again. Only yesterday the hiotion picture itself was a kind of novelty. With rapt attention we observed: "The picture moves !" It doesn't hurt our eyes ! "Things look so real!" "How clever the photographer is!"

Today the mechanical devices of story telling on the screen are still new. The devices of leaders, cut-ins, close-ups, flash-backs, visions, dissolving views, fade-outs, fade-ins, double exposures, dual roles, etc., have a strong appeal of novelty. I In the light of his experience the spectator recognizes these processes as new; and he is eager to see the next play released because it may contain some new evidence of the mechanician's ingenuity.

Novelty of physical content appeals to the spectator as well as novelty of physical form. He eagerly satisfies his curiosity with regard to other places and climes, other people and phases of life than those with which he is familiar. The South Dakota cowboy finds novelty in the story which is laid in a Cape Cod fishing village or on board a millionaire's yacht. The child of the Ghetto finds the same novelty. The fisherman, the colonial dame, and the heiress find novelty in the bitter story of the Ghetto, or in the spacious drama of the South Dakota ranches. It matters Uttle that these scenes may be "faked" by the producer of the film. The satisfaction of curiosity still takes place in the mind of the spectator. In fact, the illusion of the screen is so great that for the time the spectator feels that he is in direct contact with the reality. The impression will remain; and in the confused memory of old age this same spectator, though he has never traveled, will say, "When I was in Yokohama" — or "When I stood before the sphinx" — only to be interrupted by some indulgent grandchild who will explain, "You know, granddaddy was never there at all ; he only saw those things in the movies !"

Curiosity concerning surface structure of a play and its physical content can always be successfully appealed to by the photoplaywright. But he will never find the crowd very much interested in the abstract principles and laws upon which a play is built. It has. no critical appreciation of craftsmanship. The trained cinema composer may show commanding ability in his mobilization of humian materials for the play ; he may show keen logic in the motivation of his action ; he may show economic originality in dramatizing his pictorial setting; he may show great deftness in his plot weaving, and the crowd will sit through it all without a single aesthetic thrill. Aesthetic appreciation of workmanship is the result not of impulse but of analysis ; and the play must become established as a public favourite before these values are discovered and admired. After a play has reached the public its chances of becoming a classic are multiplied by good craftsmanship; but good craftsmanship as such is of little value in helping the play to reach the public. Therefore it would be stupid for a photoplaywright to say, "It's strange this play didn't win the crowd; I'm sure it's perfectly constructed." In other words, craftsmanship is a means and not an end, as far as the audience is concerned. The author must design and contrive deftly, almost secretly, to please the senses and capture the emotions and add to the intellectual possession of the audience. The results are paramount, while the ingenuity and artistry of the methods will either be ignored or unrecognized. But, to return to our theme, the primary intellectual experience of the spectator during a photoplay is the satisfaction of curiosity, curiosity as to content, and curiosity as to the photographic devices of telling the story.

Another intellectual process is the recognition of comic value. We are amused when we are surprised into observing an incongruity, an example of human unfitness; we laugh because we know better. In a flash we compare the unfitness of the thing with what we know should be its fitness. This comparison is a momentary, subconscious intellectual process. To be sure, the tax on our subconscious judgment is very slight. It is almost absent in our appreciation of slapstick buflfoonery. It is greatest in our appreciation of comedy of subtle or whimsical situation. In making comparisons between fitness and unfitness we naturally choose ourselves as examples of the former and the dramatic victims as examples of the latter. Thus we are more dignified than the clown who makes grimaces; we are more comfortable than the teacher who sits down upon a tack; we are more self-controlled than the talkative drunkard; we are wiser than the idiot who fears a stuffed bear ; we are more sophisticated than the country lout who tries to mail letters in the fire alarm box. This sudden recognition of personal superiority pleases us to the point of laughter. A sensation of pleasure and a feeling of hilarity sets in, which sweep the cobwebs of care from our brains. The slight, almost neglible, mental effort of recognizing incongruity relieves the brain of all mental strain, the seriousness of real life is forgotten, and we abandon ourselves to the caprice of the sportive unreality on the screen.

It must be remembered that the motion picture makes its appeal primarily through the eye. Hence it is only natural that the individual of the crowd, with his lowered intellectuality, should respond more easily to caricature of physical appearance and action than to the humour of situation which must be inferred from grasping the dramatic significance of the characters and their activities in the plot. In a following chapter we shall take up a more careful discussion of comedy in general and the possibilities of screen comedy in particular. Suffice it to say here that audiences are fond of comedy, and that they respond primarily to the kind of comedy which can be grasped visually, instantaneously, and with the least mental effort.

The process of comparison and judgment which we have just said is present in comic appeal, is a subconscious process of the mind. The opportunity of deliberately judging and reasoning would not be welcomed by the audience. The theatre crowd is neither willing nor fitted to weigh evidence and come to conclusions concerning questions of debate. The crowd is sentimental rather than philosophic. The crowd wants to see the lovers reunited at the end of the play; but it does not care to apportion the rewards of these characters according to the principles of absolute equity and justice. The crowd thrills at the proposition that no man shall treat his wife as though she were a mere chattel; but it would not warm up to a screen discussion of property rights. The crowd cheers the Stars and Stripes or a picture of the President; but it remains cold towards the tariff. The explanation of all this is that law, social science, and statesmanship require close application of thought and are only mildly diverting : and the audience wants the maximum of entertainment with the minimum of thinking. Mental receptivity is determined by mood; and the mood for visual pleasure and emotional thrill is not the mood for argument. The scenario writer must not infer from our discussion that his play may safely be brainless, but, on the other hand, he must not hope to impress the theatre crowd by the originality of his thinking, nor must he look to the photoplay as an easy medium for argumentative expression. It is true that, if he expects to reach the public and to hold it permanently, he must make the underlying philosophy of his composition sound and valid, but he must also see to it that this philosophy is underlying and not outstanding; because he cannot feed the crowd with philosophy unless he incases it in the sugar coating of emotional entertainment. The most intense intellectual experience of the spectator during the exhibition of a photoplay is the state of suspense concerning the outcome of any given situation or of the plot as a whole. Mental suspense is the fundamental element of dramatic appeal, and no play could hold the interest of an audience without it. How to arouse and maintain suspense is so important a question that we shall devote a separate chapter to its discussion. Let us merely say here that suspense is a combination of emotional and intellectual experience. The spectator is in a state of thrill and wonder regarding the progress of action; at the same time he matches his wits with the author, playing the role of detective and prophet, and tries to forecast and anticipate the action. He observes alertly every detail of the plot and makes rapid inferences concerning the content of the pictures yet to be flashed on the screen. His attention is firmly fixed until the end of the action comes, when a mental relaxation sets in, which is as pleasant as rest after bodily exertion. Without suspense a photoplay is merely a succession of pictures, and can no more hold the unwavering attention of the spectator than a row of pictures on a museum wall. Such a play displeases the individual of the audience because it deprives him of the intense mental joy of being kept in a state of doubt, anxiety, and expectation concerning the progress and outcome of a dramatic action.

Suspense is a quick, cold process of the mind, but it is also a warm state of the heart; if it were not, the crowd, being highly emotional, would never desire It. Suspense, as we have said above, is dependent on social emotions, on a definite personal sympathy with the characters in the play, and a warm interest in their careers and fates.

The individual in the crowd is willing to think providing he may think with his heart. He is also willing to think providing he may think as he pleases. There is no intellectual activity easier and more restful than the play of fancy. It is easy because it is not constrained by law; the individual may let his mind rove where it pleases. It is restful because it gives him a refreshing escape from the hard, prosaic facts of everyday life. Since the spectator enjoys the exercise of his imagination the cinema composer should spare no effort to provide him with an opportunity for this mental exercise. The fascinating thing about the motion picture is that, although to a certain extent it robs the imagination by presenting photographically to the body's eye things which had hitherto been seen only by the mind's eye, yet it admits of many entirely new means and methods of appealing to the imagination. It will be interesting to analyze and illustrate in following chapters the possibilities of appealing to the spectator's sense of wonder as well as to his imagination in new ways through the medium of the motion picture.

Thus we have studied and tried to understand the nature and mood, the affections and aversions, the whims and reliabilities, the emotional impressionability and intellectual receptivity of the average crowd in the motion picture theatres. After the cinema composer has some notion of the psychology of the crowd, after he knows pretty clearly what his aim is to be, he may more intelligently decide upon his methods for accomplishing that aim. We are now facing our problem; let us try to discover the best methods of solving it. Let us learn how best to please the eye, how to stir the self-emotion of the individual in the crowd, how to arouse and maintain his social sympathies, how to give him intellectual entertainment without mental fatigue; and let us constantly remember that if our photoplay is to become a classic it must possess beneath the attractive surface which appeals to the crowd the permanent values of illuminating truth, universal meaning, and unfading beauty.

***

Source : Victor Oscar Freeburg, *The art of photoplay making*. New York : Macmillan Company, 1918.

Frédéric Gimello-Mesplomb is a Professor of Information and Communication Sciences, Media and Cultural Studies at the University of Avignon, France. His research focuses on Media economics and audience studies. He has been a Visiting Scholar at the University of California, Berkeley, and Los Angeles (1999) and has been elected from 2001 to 2003 Faculty member of the National Academy of Television Arts & Sciences (Emmy Awards, USA). He has also served as a Visiting Professor at various international institutions (Italy, 2010; Florida, USA, 2010; Poland, 2011; Colombia, 2012; Tunisia, 2014). His work investigates the effects of public support on cultural consumption, such as emerging film and cultural funds. He delves into the evaluation methods and criteria used by Select Committees for supporting the Arts, incorporating empirical policy-relevant research that spans cultural norms and quality assessment over time within public funding frameworks. His research also examines the characterization of popular culture audiences and the consumption patterns of artistic-cultural goods.

www.ingramcontent.com/pod-product-compliance
Ingram Content Group UK Ltd.
Pitfield, Milton Keynes, MK11 3LW, UK
UKHW042015290726
14061UKWH00001BB/17

9 791043 111785